English History

A Concise Overview of the History of England from Start to End

Eric Brown

Text Copyright © Eric Brown

Legal & Disclaimer

The information contained in this book and its contents is not designed to replace or take the place of any form of medical or professional advice; and is not meant to replace the need for independent medical, financial, legal or other professional advice or services, as may be required. The content and information in this book has been provided for educational and entertainment purposes only.

The content and information contained in this book has been compiled from sources deemed reliable, and it is accurate to the best of the Author's knowledge, information, and belief. However, the Author cannot guarantee its accuracy and validity and cannot be held liable for any errors and/or omissions. Further, changes are periodically made to this book as and when needed. Where appropriate and/or necessary, you must consult a professional (including but not limited to your doctor, attorney, financial advisor or such other professional advisor) before using any of the suggested remedies, techniques, or information in this book.

Upon using the contents and information contained in this book, you agree to hold harmless the Author from and against any damages, costs, and expenses, including any legal fees potentially resulting from the application of any of the information provided by this book. This disclaimer applies to any loss, damages or injury caused by the use and application, whether directly or indirectly, of any advice or information presented, whether for breach of contract, tort, negligence, personal injury, criminal intent, or under any other cause of action.

You agree to accept all risks of using the information presented inside this book.

You agree that by continuing to read this book, where appropriate and/or necessary, you shall consult a professional (including but not limited to your doctor, attorney, or financial advisor or such other advisor as needed) before using any of the suggested remedies, techniques, or information in this book.

Table of Contents

Introduction

The history of England is just as interesting as its land and people. It's a long and winding summary of accounts relating to its centuries of struggle, turmoil, upheavals, and scandals. Although to an outsider, it's interesting to note that England's history was formed by a violent autocratic powerplay among long lines of dynasties and anarchy exhibiting their greed for power and bloodshed, still everything had helped formed what England is today.

Even what seems to be an unending battle of wills between the state and religion is another factor that's noteworthy along with the long lists of women who played significant roles in major events which had contributed much to the development of its culture.

The history of England, just like the history of any nations revealed to us the constant fight for supremacy among those in power which had not only sacrificed so many lives - especially of people born with less luck if not the lack of it.

It's sad to note that the authority given unto these people along with many lives that were put into their hands were exploited and rummaged while they go after their own personal whims and schemes. As history unfurls itself before our eyes, it showed us that even religion was only a tool for those who seek for power but was not lucky enough to take the throne. There's really no difference between these two superpowers. In fact, they share the same goal which is to rule the world at the expense of the land and people.

Regardless of the countless bloodsheds and sacrifices of many who were regarded as a pawn in their persistent powerplay, the constant struggle always leads to a change and it's this changes which brought humanity to where it is now.

Despite the many losses in the past, England remained to be a symbol of power and wealth. Even as England has become more diverse culturally, it continues to exert a strong cultural influence on the rest of the countries all over the world. English literature, arts, and culture are still enjoying a wide audience overseas, and the English language remains to be the preferred medium of communication in many parts of the globe especially in the world of business.

Chapter 1: Prehistory and Antiquity

The English prehistory includes massive spans of time, so archeologists at that time divide history into three major periods.

- Stone Age
- Bronze Age
- Iron Age

Each of these periods was further subdivided. Take for example the Stone Age which was further subdivided into:

- Paleolithic (Old)
- Mesolithic (Middle)
- Neolithic (New Stone Age)

Archeological findings and the use of cutting-edge technologies including DNA, Isotopic, and chemical analyses along with the new ways of interpreting carbon dating all helped in overturning old certainties while challenging long-held ideas and raising new questions about the fascinating pre-historical events in the history of England.

The Early Dwellers

The Ice Age

Some archeologists working in an area near Happisburgh in Norfolk were able to uncover flint tools dating back to about 900,000 years ago. These tools were used by hominoids who would periodically visit Britain during warmer eras between Ice Ages. At this time, Britain wasn't even an island but a peninsula of the Continent of Europe.

So far, the oldest human remain found in England dated back to 500,000 years ago of a six-foot-tall species of Homo Heidelbergensis. Based on archeological studies, the Neanderthals who were shorter and stockier visited Britain between 30,000-35,000 years ago. Following them were the direct ancestors of the modern human race.

The people during the Ice Age created the earliest known cave art in England about 13,000 years ago at Creswell Crags in Derbyshire.

The Stone Age

Hunters and Gatherers (9500-4000 B.C.)

As the climate improved at the end of the Ice Age, people in Britain were preoccupied with hunting and gathering of food. Although these people were generally nomadic, recent discoveries showed that some had settled lifestyle. Around 6500 B.C., the rising water level had buried the land bridge connecting to Europe leaving behind Britain as an island.

Over a thousand years ago, the first group of people that settled in England were from Europe. They were Stone Age hunters living all over Europe and the British Isles. It was around 2400 BC when a group of farmers arrived in England from Southern Europe. These people built the mysterious stone monuments including the Stonehenge.

In about 1700 B. C., another group of invaders came. These people were taller and stronger. They came from Germany and Holland and were using metal tools. Like all the settlers who came before them, they mixed and married with the natives.

10

First Farmers (4000 B. C.)

Farming was first introduced in England around 4000 B. C. by people from Europe who traveled by boat. They planted barley, wheat, and pulses, but people at that time still relied mainly on wild food and resources. Because Neolithic and Early Bronze Age people were used to hunting, instead of settling in one place, they moved around within territories. Such territories were focused on communal monuments. Some of these were gathering places while others were burial sites.

Sacred Landscapes (3500-2300)

During the Middle up to the late Neolithic era, there were new types of monuments which appeared including timber circles like Woodhenge at about 2300 B. C. Stone circles like Castlerigg in Cumbria appeared at around 3000 B. C. There were also earthwork henges like the Knowlton in Dorset. Sometimes, henges and circles are combined such as those stone circles at Avebury and Stone henge which were both estimated to be built about 2500 B. C.

In some other places, there are several types of monuments that were built in the same area over long periods like those sacred landscapes at Avery, Stonehenge, and Marden Henge. It is somewhere during this time when flint tools and weapons were first discovered at Grime's Graves in Norfolk.

Bronze Age

The first metal and jewelry reached Britain along with the new kind of pottery known as Beaker. When people died in the early days, these objects were buried along with them. Initially, metals used were made of copper but later - about 2200 B.C. bronze was introduced.

Iron Age

From the early - middle Iron Age, people began to make tools and weapons out of iron in addition to building bigger and elaborated hillforts like the Old Oswestry in Shropshire and Maiden Castle in hillforts. There were likewise many pieces of evidence recovered suggesting the dominance of a warrior aristocracy and emergence of tribal territories at that time.

It was during the late Iron Age that tribal centers were created and emerged such as Stanwick Iron Age Fortifications, North Yorkshire and Lexden Earthworks, Essex. It was also during this period that they deal with the Romans, and this became the beginning of the famous entry in English history as a result of their contacts with the Greeks and Romans. Famous among these accounts were those of Julius Caesar who raided Britain in 55-54 B.C. Accounts during this period include chariot warfare and the Druids - who were religious leaders who were said to have worshipped in oak graves and performed sacrifices. After a hundred years from the time of Caesar's raids, Emperor Claudius ordered for the invasion of the British territory.

The first metal and jewelry reached Britain along with the new kind of pottery known as Beaker.

The Celts

The Celts first step foot in England in about 800 B.C. They came from Germany and France. Another group of Celts who were fierce warriors came in the 4th century invading lands in the north of England and Ireland. They were the first group of the aristocracy to control a large part of Britain. They imposed the Gaelic language on the people which up to now are still used to some degree in Scotland, Ireland, and Wales.

The Romans

After the Celts were the Romans. They first came in 55 and 54 B. C. They lived peacefully in England for about 300 years and introduced a highly developed legal system - the system of taxation, engineering skills, the Latin language, and Roman architecture.

In the fourth century, Rome was converted to Christianity. To spread religion, Christian missionaries traveled to England. We call this period Celtic-Roman period because the two groups were able to live peacefully.

In the 4th century, at the time of the collapse of the Roman Empire, the Roman troops left England to go back to their place. There were disagreements among historians regarding the contributions of the Romans to the History of England. While others because their contributions were great, others believed it was indeed very minimal.

But after the Romans had left, the remaining Celtics were invaded by another group - the Anglo Saxons who played a significant role in English History.

Chapter 2: Medieval England

Norman Legacy

King Henry II became the King of England in December 1154 following anarchy and a Civil War of Stephen's reign. Though Stephen had sons that might succeed him, these sons were not able to reign in their father's stead. Eustace, Stephen's eldest son, died in 1153 while his younger son lived as count of Mortain. While primogeniture was not then established in England, Stephen acknowledged Henry II as his heir- designate to the throne of England.

Grandson of Henry I of England, young and vigorous Henry II became king on December 1154 and succeeded the civil war and anarchy of Stephen's sovereignty. Under him and his sons' (Richard I and John) kingship, Britain experienced fast uprising population, establishments of new towns, forest clearances for fields, and outward-looking crusading enthusiasm. Britain also attested to the 12th-century renaissance in arts and cultural festivals demonstrated by the Winchester Bible of c.1160 which was made from 300 calves' skins and extravagantly decorated with gold and lapis lazuli applied by a team of manuscript illuminators from continental Europe.1066 Norman invasion legacies remained.

Bruce, Balliol, and Wallace- families of French origin- that were dominant in Scottish medieval history became a minority that overlaid Scott population. Until after 1350, the aristocrats spoke French. For instance, the Saxon 'ox' and 'swine' were called 'boeuf' and 'porc' in French. England's north of Saxon (Sassenach) - normalized lowland of Scotland stayed disparate from the highlands where Gaelic flourished though both shared a common vernacular dialect with the north of Humber, England. Meanwhile, Ireland also was less dominated by the Normans. Despite Norman aristocracy and monarchy, majority of the indigenous regional culture still existed.

English Nationalism

There were external factors that contributed to making England more dissonant and inward-looking after 1200.

The Moslem recapture of Jerusalem in 1187 and the Battle of Hattin made a serious blow to Western hopes of international crusading ideals. Subsequent to this was also discouraging because in his campaign against Saladin, Richard I failed to recapture the city. In 1204, crusading ideals were fractured due to the siege and capture of Christian Constantinople led by a Venetian crusading force that was originally destined for infidel Egypt. Finally, crusading ideals were extinguished.

English barons declared anti-foreign attitudes as they became more conscious of their nationality. Soon after 1200, French lands were lost to John that frustrated and made England more country-conscious. As the population increased in the 1200s, many younger warrior sons looked for lands and glory. Primogeniture became more appealing and established.

Henry III (1216-1272)

King Henry III was not a militant king, and it was evident in his half-hearted campaigns in regaining lost lands in France by his father, King John. He conceded his claims to northern France and iconic Normandy by signing the Treaty of Paris in 1259 and secured remote Gascony. His reign induced closer links with France when Louis IX (St. Louis) became his brother-in-law. Thus, French culture was reverberated especially in Gothic architecture, in Britain.

Even though French names and manners were promulgated, English barons declared anti-foreign attitudes towards immigrant courtiers as they were increasingly conscious of their own nationality. In fact, the spare, simple Gothic architecture of the 13th century was also called

'Early English' by scholars, and the Salisbury Cathedral (built between 1220 and 1258) served as its epitome.

Edward I (1272-1307) and the English Government

During the 13th century, dominant English crusading continued. When the father of Edward I died in 1272, he was away crusading for two years.

Due to effective government administration in England, smooth transitions occurred. Centralized financial record keeping of the great roll of exchequer still functioned and remained unbroken early in the reign of Henry II. Indications of less dominant monarchy and tributes to growing institutions of the English government were accepted in this era:

Scotland recovered the Western Isle. England proved that expansionism was not the only way to preserve the country. Though absent for almost the entire period of his reign, Richard I realm was governed successfully.

Henry III succeeded his unpopular father at the early age of 9 and reigned for almost 10 years. The power transition from Henry III to Edward I while Edward I was gone for 2 years crusading.

Even though the financial organization was effective, some disadvantages also occurred.

- Peasant agriculture prospered.
- Urbanism grew.
- Rapid population growth.

These meant that during the 13th and 14th century, England could focus on Wales, Scotland and the lesser part of Ireland - its nearest neighbors.

When some parts of Wales were subdued by Edward I, he focused on building great castles in Wales by using his government's wealth. Through this, North Wales was put under his power.

On the other hand, the Western Isles were regained by Scotland from Scandinavian colonists subsequent to the Battle of Largs in 1263.

Another opportunity arose for England because of Alexander III of Scotland's untimely death due to a riding accident in 1289. This enabled England to get involved in the center of Scottish politics as Edward I was called to judge various claimants to the throne of Scotland.

His pre-eminence was shown in a contemporary manuscript illumination that portrayed him at the center of Prince Llewelyn of Wales (right) and Alexander, King of Scotland (left).

The Anglo-Saxons

It is said that the Roman Period in Britain ended in the year 410. It was during that time when the Roman Emperor Honorius told the Britons to look after their own defenses since the Roman Empire itself was suffering from constant attacks from the nearby barbarian kingdoms. Because of this, the Roman rule over the British land faltered, giving the nearby people from Northern Germany and Southern Scandinavia as well as the Vikings in the north the opportunity to dominate the entire territory. As of today, these immigrants became known as the Anglo-Saxons.

Known to be strong warriors, the Anglo-Saxons conquered southeast Britannia in year 450 and expanded their domain from there for over six centuries. During that time, England, as we know now, is still not in existence, though it is recorded that the one found by Anglo-Saxons was a heptarchy, meaning that the land is divided into seven petty kingdoms, each ruled by a different king. These seven petty kingdoms are the following: Wessex, Essex, Mercia, Northumbria,

Kent, Sussex and East Anglia. According to Henry of Huntingdon's Historia Anglorum, these kingdoms are medieval when it comes to historiographical traditions.

The rule of the seven petty kingdoms did not come without risks; however, In order to maintain it, they did lots of power struggles against the Vikings, who eventually defeated them through numerous territorial raids. This forced them to concede before the power of various Danish kings, most notably Canute (also known as Cnut or Knut), who managed to rule an empire in England as well as in Norway and Denmark, his own country.

During the ninth century, the country was divided between the Anglo-Saxons and Anglo-Danes through various Viking invasions, resulting in the rise of Old Norse language in provinces that were invaded. It was during the eleventh century that England became part of the Danish crown, which lasted until the Norman Invasion of the year 1066.

Origin

According to Bede, a Northumbrian monk who wrote about the tribe some centuries after wrote that the Anglo-Saxons were actually 'immigrants' from Southern Scandinavia and Northern Germany. Right after the fall of Roman Empire in Europe, the Celtic tribes resumed fighting against each other, making one of the local chieftains to hire help from those immigrants, which are composed of Angles, Saxons, and Jutes. However, when the war between Celts is over, the immigrants did not return to their homeland. Instead, they started claiming the entire territory for themselves, fighting and pushing the Celtic tribes north towards Scotland, west towards Ireland and south towards Wales.

On the other hand, the Frisians, Franks and the Batavi tribes traveled by boat to Britannia through the North Sea and the English Channel. Eventually, the occupied lands became known as England, meaning

'Land of the Angles.'

Once settled, the Anglo-Saxons merged together and formed their own towns, which eventually became kingdoms. By the 9th century, all territories in England except Scotland were unified into four different Anglo-Saxon kingdoms, namely: Wessex, East Anglia, Northumbria, and Mercia. The kingdoms of Essex, Sussex, and Kent were added to their number at a later date.

The Vikings (793 - 1066)

Also known as Norsemen, Osemen or simply Nords, the Vikings rose into power during the year 793 or late 8th century. Vikings are well-known for their ferocity as well as being battle-hardened warriors. The most memorable about Vikings, however, is none other than their raiding activities.

The primary target of these raids is monasteries since these places are rich with provisions, valuable treasures as well as potential slaves. The first-ever record of a monastery experiencing a Viking raid is during the year 793 when the Vikings raided the monastery in Lindisfarne, a place in the northeast coast of England.

Origin

Unlike the popular belief, the Vikings aren't a particular Scandinavian tribe. Instead, it is a collective name for a group that is usually composed of sons of Scandinavian and Northern Germanic royalty or nobility. Having inherited nothing from their parent's estate, these sons banded together with other fierce warriors like themselves and decided to leave their homeland. Known to be excellent sailors and traders, the Vikings usually raid places of value such as properties belonging to the Ecclesiastical community (e.g., Monasteries, Abbeys, and Churches) as well as towns, cities, and villages.

At first, the Viking raids only last for a few days or weeks per year before they return to their homelands to sell their booty. In addition to that, those raids are usually done by one or two longboats and a cargo vessel for carrying off booty. However, when the raids became known to be a very profitable business for Vikings, their activities also intensified and became widespread throughout Europe as well as in some parts of Asia. Eventually, their numbers increased to more than ten longboats and the raids last for months. Needless to say, the places the Vikings had raided during that time were literally 'shaved' from head to toe.

Culture

Since Saxons and Vikings came from the same places, they also happened to share similar traditions and beliefs despite their slight differences in language. Their gods happened to be the deities in Scandinavian or Norse Mythology, of whom Odin (for Vikings) or Wotan (for Saxons) or Woden (for Anglo-Saxons) is the chief. When it comes to technology, Vikings are unrivaled when it comes to their navy, as evident by their so-called 'longboats' and Knarr, their sea vessel for carrying off cargo.

Having reached its peak of development during the 9th century, the Viking Longboat is a shallow, long and narrow vessel. Optimized mainly for speed, the longboat is also capable of traveling rivers and coastal waters that can easily destroy other sea vessels. As a part of their custom, the longboats include finely-carved figureheads of mythological beasts in order to identify its owner or captain. In addition to that, the Viking longboat's keel and hull are reinforced with iron so that it can ram right into enemy ships with ease. They also use an instrument that is similar to astrolabe as well as caged crows. Pretty symbolic of the two crows that bring news to Odin, the Viking's caged crows are specially-trained to find land wherever they go.

The Normans (1066 - 1154)

Right after the Vikings, Normans, an ethnic group that originated from Normandy in Northern France, dominated England.

Origin

Even though the Normans that invaded England in the year 1066 came from Normandy, their origins can be traced back to Vikings from Scandinavia that raided the land until the 8th century. Unlike the other Vikings who usually terrorize coastlines and gathering profits from their collected booty, these 'Proto-Normans' decided to settle down and cultivate the land that they claimed for themselves. They also traded goods and shared knowledge with their neighbors peacefully until they eventually embraced their neighbors' traditions, which led them to abandon Paganism and embrace Christianity.

At the beginning of the 10th century, Charles the Simple of France decided to give some lands in Northern France to Rollo, a distinguished Viking Chief during that time. He did this since he thought that such a gesture would stop the Vikings from raiding French territory. By accepting the land, Charles the Simple hoped that the Vikings will join the feudal economy and will serve him in times of war. The land that he gave became known as Northmannia, which means "Land of the Northmen." It was then shortened to Normandy later.

By doing such thing, Charles the Simple managed to protect his own territory from the terror of the Vikings since these 'Proto-Normans' decided to initiate their raids elsewhere in respect for his goodwill. They also intermarried with the French, so they all became French-speaking Christians by the year 1000. However, they also started conquering territories in Italy in the year 1030. They were known to have taken over most of Southern Italy sixty-nine years later.

Culture

Well-known for being devout and pious Christians, Normans are remembered best for their achievements in the Crusades as well as displaying remarkable skill in governing territories, especially in Italy. They also established many churches, cathedrals, and monasteries for spreading Christianity as well as schools for education. After conquering England, the Normans also built many castles to defend their territory.

Chapter 3: Royal Turmoil and Successions

The Tudors are one of the most distinctive lineages in English history as Henry VII of Welsh origin significantly ended the Wars of Roses and established the House of Tudor. Henry VII and his children - his son Henry VIII, and his grandchildren Edward VI, Mary I, and Elizabeth I ruled for 118 eventful years.

It was the House of Tudor who took England's throne when he defeated Richard III - the last Plantagenet king. When King Henry defeated King Richard III of the Yorks at the Battle of Bosworth, it was the beginning of the Tudor era which lasted until the death of Queen Elizabeth I in 1603.

Henry VII, a Lancastrian laid the foundations of his dynasty and brought an end to the civil strife of the Wars of the Rosea. By his marriage to Yorkist heiress, Elizabeth of York, he was able to securely establish the Tudors to the throne of England.

During the reigns of three generations under the Tudor monarch, England underwent huge changes as Henry VIII ushered in a new state religion. The increasing confidence of the state goes along with the growth of an English culture distinct to them.

The English saw unprecedented upheaval during the Tudor era. The five Tudor kings and their queen introduced big changes that were brought down and were still with us until today.

The Reformation and Counter-Reformation

Henry VII (1485-1509)

Henry VII brought 85 years of civil war to a halt as he unified two factions - the Yorkists and the Lancasters and married Elizabeth, daughter of Edward IV and heiress of the York. Elizabeth bore him two sons, Arthur and Henry VIII. Callous and calculating, Henry secured his position by growing his financial base mostly at the expense of his people and controlling aristocratic powers.

Henry VIII

From the mid-1520s, the reign of King Henry was overshadowed by his need for a legitimate son to become the heir to the throne. He had a daughter by his first wife, Katherine of Aragon named Mary. Too desperate to have a son, he married Anne Boleyn but never got the papal consent for a divorce which made Henry decide to break ties with Rome. In 1533, he declared himself as the head of the Church of England and not the Pope. This decision led to the initiation of the Reformation of English religion, which was the most crucial event of the Tudor period which helped shape the history of England for centuries to come.

In line with the Reformation, Henry launched the Suppression or what was known as the Dissolution of Monasteries (1536-1940). The king and many favored subject were greatly enriched with the confiscated wealth of the monasteries.

Edward IV

With the accession of Edward VI, radical Protestant reform began as Edward himself is an enthusiastic Protestant. Despite the rising against the new Protestant Book of Common (1949) by a West Country, still, the reform intensified under Edward's Lord Protector, the ambitious Duke of Northumberland.

Crowned at the age of nine, Edward VI was the first king to be raised as a Protestant. His parents were Henry VIII and Jane Seymour. Edward was the King of England and Ireland from 1547 - 1553.

Because the former King Henry VIII had broken ties with Rome, Edward was educated by a Protestant tutor. His uncle who was his constant companion and also a Protestant encouraged the boy to make radical changes on the present. All these consequently led to his decision of dissolving chantries and seizing all their treasures. Such action was an attack on the Catholic's belief in Purgatory along with saying prayers for the dead.

Other changes as declared by the state included:

Priests were allowed to marry. However, this was opposed by the Catholics strengthening the rule of celibacy among Catholic priests and forbade them to marry. (1549)

- A new Prayer Book was introduced (1552)
- Abolition of altars and replacing them with simple tables
- Priests should not wear elaborate clothing
- Instead of the Mass, it was replaced by the Holy Communion.
- Predestination or the belief that it was already decided if you are bound for heaven or hell was accepted.
- Money can't buy you a place in heaven, good deeds, saying prayers or donating money to the church.

In 1553, Edward VI died at the age of 15. Before this Edward became ill, he bequeathed the Crown to Lady Jane Grey, a great-granddaughter of Henry Vii and Northumberland's teenage daughter-in-law. However, she managed to reign only for nine days as she was ousted by a group of enthusiasts yearning to install Mary as the legitimate heir to the throne.

Mary, the eldest daughter of Henry VIII, will be the next in line for the throne as indicated in King Henry's will. However, Sir John Dudley – the Duke of Northumberland wanted to prevent the succession of the Catholic Monarchs and announce that both Mary and Elizabeth could not take them through as they were both illegitimate and therefore chose Lady Jane Grey, the granddaughter of King Henry VIII youngest sister. And to have full control, Northumberland arranged a marriage for his son, Guildford and Lady Jane.

Lady Jane was able to serve for only nine days as Mary raise her claim to the throne. With the people on her side, she was able to take her position on the 19th of July 1553. Northumberland, Guillard, and Lady Jane were executed in 115 for treason.

Queen Mary I

Mary I was the daughter of Henry VIII and Catherine of Aragon who was called and remembered by many as "Bloody Mary." Nicknamed as such, Mary was hated by many for burning Protestants throughout the land in her bid to restore Catholicism to England.

It was in 1553 when Mary became Queen following the death of her brother Edwards and after Jane Grey was deposed. As soon as Mary was put to power, being a loyal Catholic, she immediately reversed the Reformation efforts of her father and brother before her. She executed many Protestants. Catholic fixtures and images were immediately restored, and the Parliament set the Heresy laws in 1955 proclaiming it a crime to be a Protestant and all Protestants who refused to recant their religion and be converted to Catholicism were burnt.

The first to be executed was John Rogers who was responsible for translating the Tynedale's Bible into English. Soon after, there were more who died for the sake of Protantism including The Bishops,

Hugh Latimer, Thomas Cranmer, and Nicholas Ridley. Queen Mary was responsible for burning 227 men and 56 women – mostly in the South East of England.

Mary was married to Phillip II of Spain in 1554. Phillip has joined Queen Mary in her bid to restore England to Catholicism. However, the majority of the English people were not in favor of the marriage as they have no desire to be governed by a foreigner resulting in racial tension between the Spanish and English merchants in London. About 3,000 men led by Thomas Wyatt marched in protest against the marriage of the Queen and her anti-Protestant policies from Rochester in Kent to London.

In 1555, Mary's pregnancy which was supposed to be due in the month of June was announced, but many believed it to be a phantom pregnancy which came out to be right since Mary had cancer of the womb. Mary I who was also known as "Bloody Mary" had no child and neither was her death mourned.

It was her belief that unless Catholicism was restored in England, all her subjects would go to hell. Therefore, it was Mary's primary goal to restore Catholicism in the whole of England. The land was divided into those who favored her decision and those who were against it.

Through the persuasion of Philip, Mary declared war on France, but the move proved to be disastrous for both Mary and England. It was during this war that the French invaded and was able to reclaim Calais. Calais was the last possession England had in France. This decision of Mary proves to be the last straw as the people were fed up of paying higher taxes just to finance the war that was committed to help Spain.

After her, Elizabeth I, her half-sister succeeded Mary I.

Elizabeth I

Shortly after Elizabeth was declared a successor to the throne of England in 1559, a peace treaty was signed unifying England, Spain, and France which brought peace to Europe.

Without the cost of the war to pay for, England became prosperous, and in 1568, Elizabeth chose to spend funds for the development of the navy. New ships that were faster and easier to steer were built. By the end of the year when these ships were built, the English navy seized a treasure ship of Spain bound for the Netherlands. This angered King Philip II of Spain and hurting the relationship between these two countries.

King Philip was quite annoyed with Elizabeth when she restored Protestantism in England, and his anger was further aggravated after Elizabeth made Francis Drakes as one of the knights. Among the countries of Europe, there existed an agreement at that time that there would be free trade, yet Drake referred to trade in private. When Elizabeth gave him the knighthood, Phillip saw this as an insult to the free trade agreement and therefore prepare for war.

When William of Orange, the Protestant leader of Netherlands was assassinated, Elizabeth provided Drake with 25 ships of navy with a mission to harass Spanish ships. Drake followed Elizabeth order and took possessions from Colombia and Florida. In retaliation, Phillip seized all English shops in Spanish ports.

England allied with the Protestant Dutch states that yearned for freedom from Spain and sent them the English army. Philip in return blocked the Channel and allowed the Duke of Parma to invade England.

In 1587, Elizabeth ordered for the execution of Mary Queen of Scots and Phillip planned the England invasion. However, the plan was against foiled by Drake who managed to enter Spanish waters and burn a large number of Spanish ships bound for England.

On May 28, Phillips Armada set sail from Lisbon but was forced to dock to the port Corunna when it encountered a storm. Repairs were made, and in July of 1588, the Armada was ready to set sail again.

Mary Queen of Scots (1542-1587)

Mary Queen of Scots, daughter of James V of Scotland and Mary of Guise inherited the throne when his father died at the Battle of Solway Moss. Mary was supposed to marry Edward, the only son of Henry VIII but the Scots decided to have an alliance with France which broke the marriage arrangement. In 1558, Mary married Francis, an heir to the throne and in 1559; the couple became king and queen of France.

However, their happy times together ended when Francis died in 1560. Mary refused to stay in France and therefore returned to Scotland. During her stay in France, Scotland became a Protestant country and did not want Mary who is a Catholic to have an influence.

In 1565, Mary married her cousin, Henry Stuart, Lord of Darnley, also an heir to the throne. This time, Mary's married life wasn't a happy one as Darnley was always jealous of Mary's closeness with her secretary, David Rizzio and he had him killed before Mary in 1566. Mary was then six-months pregnant with James I.

Darnley had made enemies with many Scottish nobles that in 1567, his house was blown up and his body was found strangled inside. Three months after the incident, Mary married the Earl of Bothwell who was the major suspect in the death of his former husband. This angered the Scottish that they turned against her. To escape the people, she fled to England after being removed from the throne. She appealed to Elizabeth I of England for support. Suspicious that she would raise Catholic support to take the throne of England, Elizabeth kept Mary a prisoner for 18 years. It was in 1586 that letters sent to Mary by a certain Thomas Babington, a Catholic was found revealing a plot to kill Elizabeth and replaced her with Mary. With this evidence on hand, Elizabeth could do nothing else but signed Mary's death warrant. Mary Queen of Scots was then beheaded on February 8, 1957, at the Fotheringay Castle.

With the Armada under the control of Medina Sidonia, the Spaniards approached the English Channel putting the English navy ready for defense. The defending fleet under the command of Lord Howard of Effingham included sips of Drake, Hawkins, and Frobisher. Drake captained "The Revenge while Effingham" sailed in the "Ark Royal" which was built in 1581 for Raleigh.

However, Effingham stationed a large contingent at Plymouth in the protection of the south-west coast from a direct landing instead of concentrating all his resources on the straits of Dunkirk as Phillip had known. According to some version of the history, at this point, Drake was playing a game of bowls when their troop sighted the Armada, and he chose to finish the game before setting sail.

Most of the Armada's Captains want to conduct a direct assault on England, but they were strictly forbidden by the strict order of Medina Sidonia. So, the fleet sailed on from the Lizard to Calais to meet the Duke of Parma, but the Duke of Parma was not around. So, the Armada dropped anchor to await his arrival.

At midnight of August 1588, Howard sent eight fire ships to the congested Spanish ranks sending them scampering while trying to get away from the flame only to be exposed to the waiting gunfire of the enemies. It was unlucky on the part of the Spanish that their firepower is not as powerful as those of the English troops. Added to this, nature seemed to favor the English navy as a change of wind blew the Armada North out of the firing range of the English fire. The Spanish troops were then driven further to the North by a gale, and many were dashed on the Northern rocks. Those who were left of the Spanish troops were forced to make their way around the Orkneys and down the Irish coast. What remains of the proud Armada sailed back to Spain.

Armada may not have been defeated due to English superiority as according to some findings, cannon balls found at the bottom of the North Sea has shown that Spanish cannonballs were of different sizes. There is a great possibility that the cannonballs used by the Spaniards were not of the right size; hence they were not able to fire back at the English troops and cause them to retreat.

Lady Jane Grey

Lady Jane Grey was the daughter of Henry Grey and Frances Brandon (daughter of Mary who is the youngest sister of Henry VIII) who was born in October 1537. Lady Jane was well educated and a devout Protestant. She was sent to the Court at the age of nine under the protection of Katherine Parr until the death of Henry VIII. She joined Katherine's household when Katherine married Thomas Seymour. She became Thomas ward following the death of Katherine in 1548. Seymour tried to arrange a marriage between Jane and Prince Edward but failed.

Finally, Thomas was executed for treason in 1549 when he tried to murder Edward and Jane became the ward of John Dudley. In 1551, John Dudley became the Duke of Northumberland and the chief counselor of Edward VI.

By 1552, it was apparent that Edward illness was getting worse. John Dudley realized that if either Mary or Elizabeth would succeed the Throne, his position would be in danger and since both of the ladies were declared illegitimate, Jane Grey can have a claim on the throne. Dudley then arranged a marriage for Jane and his son, Guildford.

When Edward died in 1553, he proclaimed Jane Grey as his

successor which overruled the Third Succession Act of 1543 restoring Mary and Elizabeth to the line of succession. Dudley tried to keep the news of Edwards's death in his attempt to capture Mary and prevent her from gathering support for the throne, but the people believe that Mary had the right to the throne. However, prior to Mary accession to the throne, Jane Grey was officially proclaimed Queen and officially served her function for nine days before Mary was put in place. Although Dudley attempted to overthrow Mary, her support was great, and she was formally claimed Queen on the 19th of July of the same year. Jane Grey and her husband were imprisoned in the Tower of London along with John Dudley who was finally executed on August 21, 1553.

In 1954, when Thomas Wyatt led a rebellion protesting against the marriage of Queen Mary to Phillip II of Spain, many nobles supported the rebellion calling for the restoration of Jane Grey as Queen. This forced Mary to authorize the execution of Lady Jane Grey to abort and prevent further acts of rebellion.

The Tudor Ladies – Six Wives of Henry VIII

Here are some of the women who played significant roles in England history during the Tudor era being wives of Henry VIII.

<u>Catherine of Aragon</u>

Catherine of Aragon was King Henry VIII first wife who was also the mother of Mary I. She was the youngest among the daughters of Ferdinand and Isabella of Spain and at the age of 16, she came to England in 1501 to marry Arthur, the eldest son of Henry II and heir to the throne. Catherine was formerly the Queen of Wales when she was the wife of Henry's elder brother who was then the Prince of Wales. She was only three years old when betrothed to her first husband.

Five months after their marriage, Arthur died, and Catherine subsequently married his husband's younger brother. She served as regent of England while Henry VIII won France and the English won the Battle of Flodden.

When Catherine failed to bear a child for Henry, this created serious doubts in him about his marriage. He believed that God was punishing him for having married his brother's wife and this idea was backed up by a certain passage he found in the Bible.

At this time, he had also fallen in love with Anne Boleyn, the daughter of Thomas Boleyn who recently returned to England from France. Henry was not able to divorce Catherine because she refused to grant him his wish, so Henry instead began the Reformation of England so that he could marry Anne Boleyn even without the Pope's permission. Catherine was finally divorced by Henry in 1533 and died in 1536.

Anne Boleyn

Anne Boleyn was the mother of Elizabeth and second wife of Henry VIII.

Anne, at the age of 14, along with her sister, Mary, was sent to the French court as a maid to Queen Claude. In 1522, they returned to England. Anne attracted many admirers while her sister became mistress to the King. In 1526, the King also asked Anne to be his mistress, but Anne firmly declined. This makes King Henry more determined to divorce Catherine so he can marry Anne. In 1533, they married secretly after Anne became pregnant. The king's marriage to Anne was never popular with the people as many believed she was a witch who cast in alliance with Germany a spell on the King.

When Anne's baby turned out to be a daughter, Henry was not happy with that, and that's when they started having frequent arguments. Anne became pregnant twice after the birth of Elizabeth, but both were stillborn. Wanting to get rid of Anne, Henry planted evidence showing Anne had been unfaithful and had plotted for the king's death. This led to Anne's execution in May 1536.

Jane Seymour

Henry's third wife was the mother of Edward VI. Henry became attracted to Jane who was a quiet, shy girl and was a contrast to his two previous wives. Henry married Jane eleven days after Anne Boleyn's death; he was 45 years old, and Jane was 28 years old. Henry got concerned when it took long for Jane to get pregnant but was quite happy when she gave him a son in 1538. A month later, Jane died. Before King Henry's death, his last request was to be buried next to Jane.

Anne of Cleves

Anne of Cleves was Henry VIII fourth wife. Henry mourned Jane's loss for two years. His son Edward happened to be sickly.

Having no ties with Rome, England was isolated from the rest of Europe in 1530. Henry advisers suggested that it would be a good idea for him to marry a German princess to create an alliance with Germany – another Protestant nation in Europe. Henry chose the older of the two daughters of the Duke of Cleves to be his fourth wife. The German Princess arrived in England in December 1539, but Henry was too horrified when he met her that she demanded a way out of the marriage. Unfortunately, he could not. The couple got a divorce six months after their marriage. However, Anne was well provided for during her stay in England. She died in 1557.

Kathryn Howard

Kathryn was Henry's 5th wife who was executed for adultery two years after their marriage. Henry had already chosen her before his divorce with Anne. Kathryn Howard was the daughter of Edmund Howard and cousin of Anne Boleyn. She was barely 15 years old when she was married to Henry who was 49. At that time Henry was overweight and unable to walk due to his obesity along with an injury that refused to heal.

Because Kathryn was very young and flirtatious, having an old husband bored her that she made friends among the courtiers. Unfortunately, one of the courtiers named Francis Dereham had known her affairs before her marriage to the King and blackmailed her into giving a good position in the court. This led her to be accused of adultery and subsequently to her execution in 1542.

Katherine Parr

Henry 6th wife outlived him and died in 1548. Henry married again in 1543 to Katherine Parr who has been widowed twice. She was kind and was a good stepmother to his three children and took good care of the King. After the death of her husband, she became the wife of Thomas Seymour, Edward's uncle. In 1548, Katherine died in childbirth.

Chapter 4: The Late Medieval Wars

Despite the fact that most of England had been united during the late medieval period, wars simply didn't end. Now that the country demands one single ruler over all, the members of the royal family, the nobility as well as others who want the crown for themselves continue to wage war against each other. This kind of 'politics' not only involved their own family but the populace and their entire territory as well. All in all, the wars during this time can be summed up to this one short statement: The victor takes it all.

Capetian-Plantagenet Rivalry

Also known as the First Hundred Years War and Angevin-Capetian Struggle, the Capetian-Plantagenet Rivalry is a series of disputes between the House of Capet, which rules the Kingdom of France, and the House of Plantagenet, which rules the Kingdom of England. Having lasted for a hundred years (1159-1259), this rivalry seeks to undermine and suppress the power of the Angevin Empire, which is controlled by the Plantagenet (also known as the House of Anjou).

Even if the French Sovereign is the overlord of the English during that time, the latter's continental possessions are far greater than their own. This is the main reason why the Capetian wants to control England for themselves.

Henry II (1133-1189)

Henry II (or Henry Plantagenet) founded the Angevin Empire. Being the son of Geoffrey, the Count of Anjou and Empress Matilda of England, Henry was known for having good fortune in addition to his ambition. Through the help of Treaty of Winchester (which also happened to end the anarchy during King Stephen's reign) and demand of the Church, Henry became the undisputed successor to the English throne for over a century.

By the year 1154, Henry was already a powerful king in Europe. Having married Eleanor of Aquitaine, a divorced wife of King Louis VII of France, he managed to double his territory while cutting Louis' dominion into half at the same time. In addition to that, Eleanor also bore him four sons compared to the French king's two daughters (during that time, a Queen is considered a failure and eligible for divorce if she failed to bear sons for her husband).

For two decades, Henry's reign became very fruitful. Having re-established royal authority and order in England, he became free in pursuing his ambitions for expansion. By 1173, he became the overlord of Toulouse, Vexin and Brittany, which became places of strategic importance for the country. He also made alliances with the Duke of Saxony, with Lombardy as well as Navarre and subdued Ireland.

In the mid-1160s, his political authority increased because of Assizes of Clarendon and the Constitution, whose aim is to lessen the Church influence when it comes to governing the country. This political move became a double-edged sword for him since, even though he had obtained greater authority, the Church, as well as the populace supporting the Ecclesiastical community, showed discontentment to his governance. In addition to that, his most loyal knights assassinated Thomas Becket, the Archbishop of Canterbury in the year 1170 to show him their support to his cause. However, instead of getting the populace's favor back, this only made things worse, having his own family added to the list of those who hated him.

Three years after that, Henry's sons allied themselves with the King of Scotland and some nobles along with the aid of their mother and King Louis. Their rebellion, however, was quelled due to their lack of coordination with one another. Because of this, Henry managed to overcome the threat by defeating his sons in battle. After that, he imprisoned Eleanor (for being one of the masterminds) during the rest of his reign.

His share of troubles never ended with that. In the year 1183, a sibling rivalry arose with the young Henry III and Geoffrey against their own brother Richard. With the help of the new French King Philip II, the two threatened the empire's political structure. However, the danger was abated through the death of young Henry from dysentery. Because of this, the two sons' lands became Richard's.

Three years after that, Geoffrey attempted to disrupt the throne again but was accidentally killed during a joust in a local tournament. This left the division of throne between Richard, his most gifted son, and John, his youngest and most favored one.

The sibling rivalry simply didn't end there. When war broke out between Henry and Philip of France, Richard saw his unfairness when it comes to treatment towards him and his brother John during the war with the French. Due to the fear for his life and King Philip's dubious encouragement as well as rights of inheriting his father's throne, Richard decided to go against his father. Because of this, Henry loses control of Touraine and Le Mans, eventually resulting in his agreement with Richard and Philip's terms in the month of July, the year 1189. Two days after that, Henry died because of his wounds as well as heartache.

Richard I (1157-1199)

Richard I, also known as Richard the Lionheart, was born on September 8, 1157, in Oxford, England. The third but was known to be an illegitimate son; he succeeded the throne right after the death of his father Henry II. It was then that the dispute between the houses of Capetian and Plantagenet was brought to life once again. Despite the fact that England and France had joined forces in the Third Crusade (the year 1190-1192), this only happened because King Philip of France wanted to learn Richard's techniques when it comes to warfare. After doing this, Philip returned to France early, using the excuse of having an illness. The truth is that he wanted to exploit the opportunity of Richard's absence in order to lay claim of Flanders, which was originally a French territory.

Most people adored Richard for his chivalry. However, historical pieces of evidence showed that, despite that quality, he was nonetheless a selfish ruler, a bad husband and a bad father, which is evidence of his spending the throne for a few months and leaving his kingdom just to take part in wars, neglecting his royal duties and making his treasury suffer. The only saving grace during his time is that he happened to have a great royal minister in the personality of Archbishop Hubert Walter, who effectively led the country during his absence. On the other hand, nothing good comes from his family, which is evident from his brother John's cooperation with the French king himself.

After the Angevin-Capetian Rivalry, the war between the English and French went on, this time in the form of a Hundred Years War. Started from the year 1337 and ended by the year 1453, the Hundred Years' War is a series of conflicts between the House of Valois of France and the House of Plantagenet of England. Five generations of kings from these two dynasties emerged and fought against each other, making it one of the most notable conflicts during medieval times.

The conflict started during the time the women were denied the right of succession to the French throne. When Charles IV of France died in 1328, he left no heirs, technically making Edward III of England his closest male relative. However, due to the fact that he's English, he was denied this right, making his mother and Charles IV's sister, Isabella of France to claim the French throne on his behalf. Because of this, political sentiment arose, favoring a natural-born French citizen against foreigners and man against woman. This is the reason why the French throne was given to Count Philip of Valois (later Philip VI of France), which happened to be Charles IV's cousin from his father's side.

At first, the English did not pay much attention to the matter, given the fact that their territories are much more valuable. However, their disagreements led to Philip confiscating French lands belonging to Edward. This made him decide to eventually reassert his claim to the French throne as a whole.

The battles in Crecy, Poitiers, and Agincourt declared the English as victors, convincing them to continue pouring their manpower as well as resources on the war for decades. However, the French are known to have greater resources despite having a considerably smaller land area. Because of this, the battles in Orleans, Formigny, Patay, and Castillon became a decisive victory in favor of the French, making the English lose most of their possessions on the continent permanently. These incurred losses, as well as the fact that the English invested greatly in the century-long war, became the primary causes leading to the Wars of the Roses.

The Hundred Years War

The Hundred Years War started in 1937 and lasted until 1453. It was a series of turmoil and turbulence fought between England and France over the succession of the throne. It lasted for around 116 years with many major battles - from the Battle of Crecy in 1346 to the Battle of Agincourt in 1415 was the English completely defeated by the French. Here are some major facts covered in the Hundred Years War.

After the death of Charles IV in 1328 and without a son to succeed him, the throne was left to his cousin King Phillip VI. However, there are some groups who believed that Edward III of England, being the nearest male kin of the king had stronger claim over the matter of the throne.

Edward III pressed his claim to the French throne when Phillip VI confiscated the duchy of Aquitaine from England in 1337. It was the start of the Hundred Years War.

During the medieval times, there were legalities that one king could be the vassal of another if the first had inherited titles outside his own kingdom. This was the case with the English Kings since the time William I, the Duke of Normandy conquered England in 1328.

Edward III of England was also the Duke of Guyenne which is a part of Aquitaine in southwestern France and count of Ponthieu on the English Channel. Another thing, his mother was the sister of Charles IV and that when Charles IV left no heir to the throne, Edward III considered himself to be the legitimate successor. There was another claimant though, the Count of Valois, a grandson of King Phillip III of France.

To settle the issue, a French assembly was called. It decided in favor of Phillip VI who accepted the decision. However, afraid of another king's power in his realm, he maneuvered to confiscate Guyenne in 1337. This time, Edward III once again asserted his claim to the French throne and brought an army to Flanders.

In 1346, Edward the Black Prince, son of Edward III managed to capture John II at the victory of Poitiers. Edward III was given full sovereignty over lands he formerly held while a vassal of Philip through the Treaties of Calais.

When John who was held in captivity died, awaiting the fulfillment of all provisions of the cities, his son as the crowned Charles the V refused to recognize the treaties which cause the troubling to rise once again. This time, it was the French who were on the advantage until Charles V died in 1380 which stopped progress in the reduction of the English territory.

Both countries faced internal conflicts and power struggles after 1380 which provided them uncertain peace although the possession of Flanders remained an unsettled issue. Eventually, Richard Ii who was a grandson of Edward III was deposed by another grandson - Henry II.

While in France, siblings of Charles V fought over who would be in charge of Charles VI's affairs, who became mentally ill causing him to vacate the throne.

King Henry V of England who succeeds his father after his death in 1413 took advantage of the discord which was ongoing in France at the time. He campaigned for the English claims on the French crown. Henry V found an alley in Philip the Good who is the son of John the Fearless who was assassinated by the Armagnacs. By 1942, Aquitaine and all of France north of the Loire was controlled by the Anglo-Burgundian alliance.

Everything changed for the English when King Henry died leaving behind an infant child. It was only a few weeks later when Charles Vi died which allowed his son to have the French throne as Charles VII. The turning point for the war came in 1429 which forced the English to raise its siege of Orleans by a relief force led by Joan of Arc. This led to the capture of Joan by the Burgundians and was sold to the English and executed for heresy. Philip the Good, with his firm belief that the English could never assert their authority over France which is not small without the support of native nobility, he decides to switch side in 1435, so Paris once again came under the rule of France. Charles VII was able to conquer Normandy and the whole Aquitaine in 1453 after taking advantage of the internal dynasty upheavals connected with the Wars of Rose. England was only able to retain Calais which it later relinquished in 1558.

The Hundred Years War was considered by historians as a major milestone in the development of national consciousness among those living in Europe. After a long time of successions bringing along failures and frustrations, the English finally ceased their continental intervention and instead focus on issues related to internal development.

War of the Roses

From 1455 - 1485, the House of Lancaster and the House of York engaged in a series of battles. These wars were names Wars of Roses based on their badges. The Lancastrians used the red rose as their symbol while the Yorks used the white rose.

These two groups were in constant conflict due to the following:

- Both houses - Lancaster and Yorks were both direct descendants of King Edward III
- King Henry VI, the ruling Lancastrian king, was surrounded with unpopular nobles
- There was civil unrest by the majority of the population
- Many powerful Lords established their own private armies
- The untimely mental sickness of Henry VI

When Richard III who was the last king of the Yorkists was defeated at the battle of Bosworth, only then was the Wars of the Roses put to a stop. It was Henry Tudor of the House of Tudor who finally defeated him.

Origins of the Wars

It was in 1411 when Anne Mortimer brought forth a son - Richard Plantagenet for Richard V who was the 5th Earl of Cambridge. He was the son of Edmund who was the first Duke of York and the 4th son of Edward III. Richard would have been the crowned King of England if Henry the VI died before 1453, the year when Edward, the Prince of Wales was born.

Married to the ambitious French princess Margaret of Anjou, the Plantagenet King Henry VI was a weak king. During the time, there were complex issues of rivalries and jealousies among powerful noble aristocrat. The Queen, along with her circle of nobles was identified with the Lancaster. Henry belongs to the Lancaster family. Nobles who are against the Queen and the Lancasters led by Richard, the Duke of York are Henry's cousin, also a descendant of King Edward the III who likewise had a claim to the throne of England. Their group was the Yorkists.

Henry VI suffered from periods of insanity. It was during one of these periods that Richard of York was appointed to be the Protector of the Realm which gave him the opportunity to dismiss the advisors of the Queen. Upon the King's recovery, he was summarily dismissed from office.

King Henry was not able to stop the growing conflict between the Queen's party and that of the York's Earl of Warwick. Both groups started to recruit troops and prepare them for the war. Since many of these soldiers just came back from the Hundred Years War, recruiting them was easy. These two groups then choose a badge - Red Rose for Lancaster and White Rose for York, hence the wars that came after was names Wars of the Roses.

Two years after the Hundred Years War ceased, came this dynastic civil war. There were tremendous killings and bloodshed as defeated soldiers regardless on which sides were brutally killed.

Chapter 5: Renaissance Period (16th Century)

Generally, *Renaissance* marks the point of transition from the Middle Ages (or *medieval period*) heading to the modern era. The movement started in Italy at around 1300s with the decline of the Roman Catholic doctrine and the rise of interest in the classical Greek and Roman thoughts. However, the Renaissance took place at different times in various countries as it took time for other European countries to adapt its idea and concept.

Renaissance is described as a period of economic, political, and religious changes that resonates into the areas of philosophy, science, architecture, arts, and literature. Every field of life was explored, aiming for perfection. This endeavor served as a driving force to make today's era truly modern.

Education became a crucial factor in this movement as the number of schools and universities increased. The holistic concept of a humanistic curriculum focused on classical humanities subjects like poetry, history, philosophy, and drama was readily adopted in contrast with the traditional Christian theological texts. In England, humanism was accepted through "grammar schools," and the students in these said schools were giving the best classical learning. Most celebrated intellectuals like Bacon, Shakespeare, Marlow, and Spenser received a humanist education.

Overview of the English Renaissance

In England, the Renaissance took place in 1485, two centuries after it began in Italy, to the early 17th century. Many believe that the inauguration of the Tudor Dynasty signaled the beginning of this period. However, the ideas and style of the Renaissance movement were slow to saturate England; hence, the Elizabethan Age was regarded as the true Renaissance period of England. Other historians also call the English Renaissance as the *Early Modern Period*.

The English Renaissance is quite different from its Italian counterpart. The strongest art forms of the English Renaissance were music and literature; whereas, the dominant art form of the Italian Renaissance was the visual arts.

Literature and Theater

As mentioned, England had a strong tradition of literature written in their own language which eventually progressed with the popular use of the printing press in the mid-1500s. The literary culture produced the likes of poet geniuses like Edmund Spenser, the genius behind the verse epic, *The Faerie Queen*. Soon, playwright extraordinaire like Thomas Wyatt and William Shakespeare popularized dramatic poetry. During that time, the works of poets and playwrights circulate in manuscript form for some time before they were officially published.

Of all the Renaissance plays, the English theater contributed the most outstanding legacies. It started with the opening of "The Red Lion" theater in 1567. It was followed by several permanent theaters in London such as the Curtain Theatre in 1577 and the Globe Theatre in 1599. The English theater had the widest audience ranging from the court and nobility to the general public. They had the most crowded performances in the whole of Europe having a great host of playwrights including the big shots like Ben Jonson, Christopher Marlowe, and William Shakespeare.

Queen Elizabeth I herself was a product of the Renaissance movement, having trained under Roger Ascham. She wrote poems like *On Monsieur's Departure* during the most crucial moments of her life. The Italian literature had contributed greatly to the works of William Shakespeare. Even the publication of the *Book of Common*

Prayer in 1549 and the *King James Version* (or *Authorized Version of the Bible*) in 1611 created a huge impact on how even the common people of England should think.

Here are the literary notables during the English Renaissance:

- Ben Jonson
- Christopher Marlowe
- Edmund Spenser
- Francis Bacon
- Francis Beaumont
- George Chapman
- James Shirley
- John Donne
- John Fletcher
- John Ford
- John Webster
- Philip Massinger
- Philip Sidney
- Thomas Dekker
- Thomas Kyd
- Thomas Middleton
- Thomas More
- Thomas Nashe
- Thomas Wyatt
- William Rowley
- William Shakespeare
- William Tyndale

Navigation and Exploration

The Elizabethan Age witnessed the rise of the English navy when it defeated the Spanish Armada in 1588. The event also opened ways in order to improve the navigation system through the efforts of Francis

Drake when he circumnavigated the world. Other noteworthy explorers include Walter Raleigh (established Virginia Colony), Humphrey Gilbert (discovered Newfoundland), John Hawkins, Richard Grenville, and Martin Frobisher (discovered Labrador or Frobisher Bay).

While there are numerous motives which prompted the English exploration, the men were led to set discovery voyages inspired by the Renaissance spirit. The thought of spreading Christianity among the heathen also added to the thrill of exploration. Yet, perhaps the most powerful driving force to go beyond the horizons is *commerce* wherein the eastern spices play a vital role in setting the wheels in motion.

During the English Renaissance period, people lived on salt meat during winter and salt fish during the Lent—a great contrast during medieval times when spices like ginger, pepper, cinnamon, nutmeg, and cloves were more accessible. Spices were also used to create medicines and season the wine and ale. Aside from the spices, the English were also eager to acquire dyes, perfumes, gems, drugs, gums, and different kinds of woods that can only be found in the East.

Fashion, Clothing, and Textiles

Clothing and fashion were given importance particularly in the peers of nobility and the wealthy commoners during this period. Queen Elizabeth even created new Sumptuary Laws known as the "Statutes of Apparel" to specify who could wear a particular type of clothing. For instance, only duchesses, marquises, and countesses could use gold cloth, fur, and tissue in their gowns. People under the rank of knighthood were prohibited to wear silk trimming on hats and other sundries. These set of laws were strictly observed by all.

Linen and wool were ordinary fabrics during the Elizabethan era.

Linen, in particular, is favored since it's comfortable to wear and easy to wash. During that time, people rarely washed their clothes and linen eventually turned softer with use. Each fabric had its proper use:

- *Wool* keeps the body cool during the warm weather and warm during the cold season. It's an enduring fabric that does not absorb moisture and can take dyes well.
- *Felted wool* or *fulled wool* is durable and resilient. It doesn't need hemming as it doesn't unravel.
- *Cotton* was used to blend well with linen to make Fustian and to create other fabrics.

The luxurious fashion styles portrayed we see in Elizabethan artworks were observed by the elite, nobility, and royalty in that period. Upper classes used taffeta, silk, velvet, damask, and satin together with linen and wool for their clothing. They embellish their garments with lace, gems, pearls, embroidery, braiding, borders, and ribbon trims. Hats, belts, shoes, gloves, doublets and, breeches were made of leather.

As for the colors, natural dyes were the only available kind and were usually faded through time. Brown and gray were cheaper dyes which were often used by the lower classes. Blue dye was also inexpensive but was associated with apprentices and servants. Meanwhile, the black dye from Spain was rather expensive and was often used by the Queen herself. There were two dominant red shades—the crimson and russet. The former was an expensive shade used exclusively by the members of the royal family; whereas, the latter was used as a down-to-earth hue.

Layered clothing, particularly in women, was in fashion those days— the undergarments called smock and a kirtle, the bodice, several layers of petticoats, and a cloak. This style seemed to work well with the chilly and damp climate of England.

Government

The English government was constituted by three different bodies—the monarch, the Parliament, and the Privy Council. As the monarch, Queen Elizabeth I had the power to determine most of the laws in the kingdom, but she had to consult the approval of the Parliament in order to implement taxes. The Privy Council, on the other hand, was composed of the queen's closest advisors. The members had the power to give her sound advice and recommendations. When Queen Elizabeth came to the throne, there were 50 advisors in the Privy Council but eventually reduced to a party of 11 by 1597. Meanwhile, the Parliament had two groups—the House of the Lords and the House of Commons. The former was composed of the high ranking church officials and the nobles, and the latter was made up of the representatives of the commoners.

The Censure against the Concept of English Renaissance

The word "Renaissance" pertaining to this period of transition was popularized by the Swiss historian, Jacob Burckhardt, in the 19th century. The whole concept of the Renaissance has undergone much criticism by many seasoned cultural historians, and some of them strongly argued that the idea of "English Renaissance" should have never existed in the first place. For them, the English achievements could not even compare to those of the Italians with the accomplishments of Leonardo da Vinci, Donatello, and Michelangelo as a greater part of the Renaissance visual art.

However, these historians failed to regard the contributions of English in literary history. England had already established their foothold in the field of literature two centuries before the time of Shakespeare. Geoffrey Chaucer, dubbed as the Father of English Literature, initiated the style of using the English language as a medium of literary composition instead of the popular Latin. Chaucer also translated the works of Francesco Petrarca and Giovanni Boccaccio into Middle English. Even his contemporaries, John Gower and William Langland, also utilized the English language as their medium of the composition. In the mid-1400s, author of Le Morte D'Arthur, Thomas Malory became a significant figure in the literary field.

These aforementioned factors and figures made the historians and scholars contest the claim that the Elizabethan Era was England's true Renaissance period. The world-renown creator of the *Chronicles of Narnia*, C.S. Lewis, who was also a professor of Medieval and Renaissance literature at Cambridge and Oxford once remarked to a colleague that there was actually no English Renaissance, or that if it truly existed, it failed to create an effect.

Regardless of the contradictions, one cannot deny the fact that the revolutionary era in England truly transpired and its results are being relished by the current era, not only within the English soil but anywhere all over the world.

The Protestant Reformation in England

One of the major highlights during the English Renaissance period is the Protestant Reformation which triggered the religious, cultural, intellectual, and political revolution that divided Catholic Europe. It established principles and beliefs that have helped define the continent until the current modern era.

Historians often date the beginning of the Protestant Reformation to the 1517 publication of the *95 Theses* by Martin Luther and end in the 1555 Peace of Augsburg. The period features the coexistence of Lutheranism and Catholicism in Germany up to the Treaty of Westphalia in 1648 which concluded the Thirty Years War.

The major ideas of the Protestant Reformation included the

purification of the church and the belief in the Bible—not the dictates of the Catholic tradition—should be the sole provenance of spiritual authority. The reformers, particularly Martin Luther, were able to skillfully utilize the power of the printing press to spread their beliefs and ideas to a wide audience. Martin Luther published his prolific works between 1518 and 1525.

Despite the historians dating the Reformation with the publication of Luther's *95 Theses*, England had actually started to challenge the authority of the Catholic Church during King Henry VIII's quest for a male heir.

A New Development

England and Scotland were at odds for the most part of the 16th century. However, this conflict ceased to be when a Scottish king in 1603 ascended the English throne with the charm and presence that the English ruling elite approved of. This strange turn of events was greatly influenced by the peculiarities of the Tudor dynasty that had ruled England in the sixteenth century—the religious revolution initiated by King Henry VIII for his determination to marry often in order to acquire a male heir and the equal resolve his daughter, Queen Elizabeth I, not to marry at all.

Protestantism also played an important role in shaping England during that time. Even if the English aristocracy had a little respect for the throne after the death of Elizabeth I, the determination to retain England as a Protestant nation held them together.

Henry VIII

Initially, the Tudor king defended the Catholic faith, earning him the title "Defender of the Faith." He put Cambridge and Oxford, two of the most outstanding universities, to campaign against Martin Luther. He supported the finest theologians of these universities to abolish

53

the growing thread of Lutheran "heresy." At this point, Luther's attacks created minor resonance in England.

However, the Reformation got opportune progress due to the king's personal affairs. King Henry's desperation to divorce Catherine of Aragon forced him to take extreme measures to go against his own theological conservatism.

King Henry declared that the absence of a male heir to the throne threatened the future of the dynasty and the kingdom itself. He then swiftly acted from 1532 to force the Parliament to pass the legislation that restricted the influence of the papacy in England and automatically made the monarch the new head of the English Church. Finally, in 1534, he had the absolute authority behind the English Church. He then proceeded to dissolve the monasteries throughout the kingdom and confiscated their wealth.

For the most part, the political nation was rather compliant than eager. Only a few people were prepared to defend the institutions of the old church and defy the king in the process — many received windfall profits from the sequestered church properties and monastic lands.

Edward VI

During the last years of King Henry VIII, a powerful evangelical party at Court had grown. Upon his death in 1547, the group rapidly established their foundations with the newly crowned king, Edward VI. In his short reign, the young monarch made efforts to establish Protestantism in England as modeled from the German and Swiss Reformed churches. He also established a powerful alliance with Archbishop Cranmer and the Duke of Somerset.

In the five year reign of Edward, the Reformation achieved a new English order of service, two evangelical Prayer Books, and the elimination of the Catholic paraphernalia from the churches.

Unfortunately, this short period failed to generate roots. On King Edward's death in 1553, these changes were quickly reversed by his elder sister, Queen Mary I.

Queen Mary I

In the month following her coronation, Mary immediately issued a proclamation that she would not force her subjects to follow her religion. However, she soon had the leading reformers including Thomas Cranmer, John, Bradford, Hugh Latimer, Hugh Latimer, and John Hooper arrested. She also had her first Parliament declare the marriage of her parents valid and abolished his brother's, Edward VI's, religious laws. The Catholic doctrine was restored according to the form it had taken in the 1539 Six Articles which also reasserted clerical celibacy of the priests. Due to this, married priests were then denied of their benefices.

Mary's husband, King Philip II persuaded the Parliament to repeal Henry VIII's religious laws in order for England to return to the Roman jurisdiction. It took months before the approval of Pope Julius III was granted even though the confiscated monastic lands were not handed back to the church. By the end of 1554, the Heresy Acts were revived leading to the execution of numerous 300 Protestants and the exile of about 800 wealthy and influential Protestants such as John Foxe. This goes down in history as the *Marian Persecutions*.

The first executions, death by burning at the stake, happened for more than five days in the early February 1555 including John Rogers (February 4), Laurence Sanders (February 8), and John Hooper and Rowland Taylor (February 9). The former Archbishop of Canterbury, Thomas Cranmer, was forced to witness the execution of his comrades, Bishops Nicholas Ridley and Hugh Latimer, on October 16, 1955. Queen Mary did not relent on this decision despite the condemnations from Alfonso de Castro, King Philip's own

ERIC BROWN

ecclesiastical staff and Simon Renard, an adviser. The persecutions continued until her death in 1558.

Elizabeth I

When Queen Elizabeth I had ascended to the throne in 1558, she immediately worked to reverse the works of her late sister which resulted in an insecure regime. Had the childless queen died in 1563 due to smallpox, the throne could have been handed to the Catholic Mary Queen of Scots and lead to religious civil war affecting even the neighboring lands in the continent. Even so, the remarkably confident queen together with her advisors addressed all complex domestic and foreign problems due to the restoration of Protestantism.

The issue with her legitimacy both in Catholic and Protestant perspectives was an important concern. Her illegitimacy under the English Church wasn't much of an issue compared to the Catholic claims that she was never legitimate at all. This matter alone put Elizabeth's favor in Protestantism over Catholicism.

Elizabeth and her advisors discerned the threat of a Catholic crusade against "heretical" England. To deal with this, the queen came up with a solution not to greatly offend the Catholics while staying on the favorable side of the English Protestants at the same time. However, she could never tolerate the action of the radical Puritans who were pushing for more extreme reforms.

To settle the religion, a Parliament was created in 1559 and reinstated the Protestant settlement of the late King Edward VI with the monarch as its head. However, Elizabeth impeded the full Calvinist Church recommended by some of the English exiles and foreign theologians who had returned to the kingdom upon Elizabeth's ascension. She retained Catholic elements such as the ecclesiastical vestments and the bishops. Queen Elizabeth I preferred pragmatism

56

in addressing religious issues.

The House of Commons supported the queen's proposal, but they met opposition in the House of the Lords, specifically from the bishops. Fortunately, there were many vacant bishoprics during that time including the Archbishopric of Canterbury. Due to this circumstance, Elizabeth's supporters outvoted the conservative peers and the bishops. This also led to Elizabeth being forced to accept the lesser title as the *Supreme Governor of the Church of England* instead of the more controversial title of *Supreme Head*, which many people consider inappropriate for a woman to bear.

With the new Act of Supremacy in 1559, all public officials were made to swear an oath of loyalty to the monarch as the supreme governor; otherwise, they could face the risk of disqualification from their office. The laws pertaining to heresy during the time of Mary were repealed to avoid further persecution. Simultaneously, the new Act of Uniformity was passed, making church attendance and the use of an adapted version of the 1552 Book of Common Prayer mandatory although the penalties for failing to conform were not drastic.

Chapter 6: Religious and Civil Wars (17th Century)

The Reign of James I

When the son of Queen Mary of Scots, King James VI, was also hailed as the new King of England as King James I, he began a new lineage—the Stuarts.

The newly crowned king never had the same charm as his predecessor, Queen Elizabeth I, and never delighted in the same glory as hers. Nevertheless, he had his own set of achievements. First, he ended the long war with Spain in 1604; and secondly, he was accountable for the translation of the Bible which was later called the King James Version published in 1611.

The Gunpowder Plot

The Gunpowder plot was an assassination attempt for King James and the members of his Parliament. In the late sixteenth century in England, most people were Protestants, and the Catholics were the persecuted minority. Majority of the priests faced execution as they were treated as foreign agents while the common people face appalling fines for not attending the services of the Church of England.

When King James ascended the throne, the Catholics hoped that the king would treat them favorably since his Danish wife was a Catholic. At first, James stopped all fines for recusancy but the two failed Catholic plots to kill him in 1603 angered him. He reinstated the fines in the following year (1604). Still, many Catholics gave their loyalty to King James and did not partake in violent revolutions.

There were few Catholics, however, who resorted to radical measures like Thomas Percy, Robert Catesby, Thomas Winter, John Wright, and Guy Fawkes. These five men met in May 1604 and schemed what is historically known as the Gunpowder Plot.

The group executed their devious plan with Thomas Percy renting a house situated next to Parliament Houses then proceeded to "hire" Guy Fawkes as the custodian of the rented house. Part of his caretaking responsibility is the cellar underneath the House of Lords where they kept the barrels of gunpowder. They hid the barrels amongst the firewood. They also recruited other men to partake with the conspiracy.

Unfortunately for these revolutionaries, their plot was foiled. On October 26, 1605, William Parker, Lord Monteagle, received a letter from an anonymous individual warning him not to attend the parliament. Monteagle then consulted Robert Cecil, Earl of Salisbury and one of the king's ministers, regarding the message. With that, the government had uncovered the plot and began to search the Parliament buildings including the cellar beneath the House of Lords where they discovered huge amounts firewood. When they conducted a second search around midnight, they found Guy Fawkes.

The other conspirators were found and arrested. All of them were proven guilty of treason and were sentenced to death. The leader, Guy Fawkes, was hanged on January 31, 1606. Instead of helping the Catholics gain their voice, the assassination attempt led to even harsher treatments of the Catholic minority.

Every November 5, the English would celebrate with bonfires to complete with the burning of Guy Fawkes' effigy.

Conflict with the Parliament

King James had a disagreement with the Parliament regarding the rising cost of the government and of fighting wars compared to its income. The rents from royal lands could only be raised once the lease contract ended. Therefore, the Parliament was in the advantage. The Members of the Parliament intended to disagree to the increase of lease unless the king gave in to their demands. Because of this, King James had to resort to new ways in order to raise money.

The situation became even more complicated due to the conflicts over religion since many MPs were puritans. They wanted to completely eradicate the "flaws" of the Church of England by eliminating the remaining Catholic elements retained by Queen Elizabeth during her reign. Although a Protestant himself, the King did not concede to puritan views.

King James believed in the divine right of the Kings. For him, God has chosen kings to rule and with that, he became unwilling to work with the Parliament since he believed that the absolute authority was placed upon him alone.

When King James died in 1625, he was succeeded by his son, Charles I.

Charles I

Charles I, too, believed in the divine rights of the kings. He often quarreled with the Members of the Parliament. First, he married the Bourbon Roman Catholic princess, Henrietta Maria, which was a detested act in the Puritan point of view.

King Charles had also partaken in pointless wars. In 1625, he sent an unsuccessful expedition to Cadiz. Due to all of these, the Parliament strongly criticized his policies, even resorting to the rejection of raising extra taxes to support the Spanish war. This move deeply angered the king and he went as far as to dissolve the Parliament. Without the obstruction of the Parliament, he imposed forced taxes to finance his expeditions and wars. Those who refused to pay were immediately sent to the prison without trial.

By 1628, Charles was in dire need of money due to the cost of the wars. He was then forced to call the Parliament. The Parliament took this as their advantage, so they drew up the Petition of Rights, forbidding the king to levy taxes without their consent and order arbitrary imprisonment.

The King and the Parliament continued to clash regarding the issue of religion. By law, everybody under the sovereign of England should belong to the Church of England, but there were still some practicing Roman Catholics particularly in the Northwest.

In 1629, William Laud was the Bishop of London. His views strongly oppose the Puritans and Charles fully supported him. Meanwhile, the Parliament criticized the king and William Laud. King Charles called their reaction "impertinence" for he thought that the MPs held no right to oppose him. The Parliament responded by refusing to grant the king taxes for over a year. Because of this, the King sent a messenger to announce that he was dissolving the group once again. However, before the dissolution was proclaimed, the members physically restrained the speaker until they were able to pass three resolutions about the religion and Bishop William Laud. Only after then was the Parliament disbanded. This period without the Parliament was called The Eleven Years Tyranny.

William Laud was made Archbishop of Canterbury in 1633. Determined to suppress the Puritans, he checked almost all parishes by sending commissioners. He wanted to ensure that they still observe the traditions and rules of the Church of England. The bishop went as far as to stop the Puritan lecturers of their preaching.

The Bishops' Wars

In 1637, King Charles and William Laud infuriated the Scots by proposing religious reformation in Scotland as they introduced the new prayer book. The Scots went on riots in Edinburgh. In February

1638, the Scottish ministers and nobles signed the National Covenant, a document rejecting the attempts of Charles I and William Laud to conform to the Church of Scotland in accordance with the English church governance.

Meanwhile, Charles took the disturbance in Scotland as a rebellion against him. The event triggered the 1639 First Bishops' War. Charles did not consult the English Parliament to wage war and began to raise an army. They marched to Bewick-upon-Tweed, a town on the border of Scotland. The King avoided the Covenanters, the Scottish Presbyterian movement, for fear of defeat. In the Treaty of Berwick, Charles recovered the custody of his Scottish fortresses and dissolved the Covenanters' temporary government. Instead, the General Assembly of the Scottish Church and the Scottish Parliament were placed.

The failure at the First Bishops' War deepened the diplomatic and financial crisis that Charles was facing that time. His unpopularity went rock bottom when his efforts to raise funds from Spain and continuous support for his Palatine relatives resulted in the public humiliation of the Battle of Downs wherein the Dutch obliterated the whole Spanish fleet and rendered the English navy invalid.

In the early months of 1640, Charles summoned both the English and Irish parliaments in an attempt to raise funds for the new military campaign against the Scots (later called as the "Short Parliament). By March 1640, the Irish Parliament granted £180,000 along with the promise to raise an army of nine thousand. On the other hand, the earls of Strafford and Northumberland attempted for a compromise whereby the king would forfeit ship money for £650,000. Unfortunately, all of these were deemed insufficient to create unity and agreement in the House of Commons. Charles ignored further reforms proposed by the Commons as he was still backed up by the House of Lords. The protests of Northumberland fell on deaf ears, and the Short Parliament was dismissed in May 1640.

The Second Bishops' War happened in August 1640 when the Scots invaded England and seized Newcastle. Emboldened by what happened in the English Short Parliament, the Scottish Parliament declared that it could govern its own kingdom without the English King. The Covenanter army moved into Northumberland.

The English army cannot be compared to that of the Scottish which comprised of many Thirty Years' War veterans. There was no resistance at all until the Battle of Newburn. The Scots occupied the city, its neighboring county, the Durham.

It was inevitable for the king to call for the Magnum Concilium (or the Great Council), an assembly of the wealthy landowners and church leaders to discuss relevant issues concerning the kingdom. The council strongly advised for the restoration of the Parliament while Charles asked the council to help him obtain army funds against the Scots for the meantime.

England faced another humiliating blow in the Treaty of Ripon in October 1640, wherein the king signed for the cessation of arms. The treaty also stated that the Scots could have Durham and Northumberland and would be paid £850 per day until the English Parliament is restored.

Desperate for the money, Charles called the Long Parliament in November 1640. Out of the 493 members of the Commons who returned, 350 opposed the king. The Parliament soon passed the Triennial Act which stated that an assembly must be called every three years and the Dissolution Act which declared that the parliament could not be arbitrarily dissolved without its concession. Furthermore, it would be illegal to fine people who have not achieved knighthoods and landowners who had intruded on royal land, and the ship money was also abolished.

The Parliament also passed an act against the king's loathed adviser and First Earl of Strafford, Thomas Wentworth (notoriously known as "Black Tom Tyrant" during his rule as Lord Deputy of Ireland), declaring him guilty of high treason. Charles was forced to sign the act since he worried about his and his family's safety. Wentworth was executed on May 12, 1641, on Tower Hill.

Due to the drastic measures, the Parliament had been taken (mostly by the opposition led by John Pym); some MPs began to realize that they were going too far. Disharmony soon became apparent amongst the group.

The Grand Remonstrance, an anti-Catholic list of grievances setting 204 points of objection to the King's policies, a call to purge officials, the expulsion of bishops from the Parliament, and an end to the sale of land seized by the Irish rebels. Pym demanded that the king should let the Parliament control the militia. Many considered that this was an opening to something more dangerous than what Charles had been doing.

The country was beginning to be critically divided with some wanting to return the Church of England back to its state before William Laud. Others conceded to Pym's proposal of completely abolishing the bishops.

The king made the situation worse by forcing his way to the Commons and trying to arrest five Members of the Parliament (Sir Arthur Haselrig, John Hampden, Denzil Holles, William Strode, and John Pym) for high treason. However, the accused already slipped away by boat even before the king appeared. The botched arrest caused outrage as no English sovereign had ever dared to set foot on the Commons before and this was an explicit assault to the parliamentary privilege. All the efforts of his supporters to build his image as the country's defender against disorder all crumbled down. Charles was then forced to flee to Hampton Court Palace on January 10, 1642, then to the Windsor Castle two days later.

In March 1642, the Parliament then proclaimed that its ordinances were valid laws, requiring no royal agreement. Meanwhile, the king traveled northwards after sending his wife and eldest daughter abroad. In April, Charles tried to seize the military arsenal at Hull but the town's Parliamentary governor, Sir John Hotham, refused to grant him access. The king was forced to withdraw in York where he assembled the courts of justice, and his loyalists from both houses joined him.

The English Civil War

In the mid-1642, both Parliamentarians and Royalists began to arm. Charles raised his army using the medieval strategy, commission of array while the Parliament assembled volunteers for its militia. On August 22, the king raised his royal standard in Nottingham, signaling the start of war after the failed negotiations with the Parliament (also known as The Nineteen Propositions).

At the beginning of the First English Civil War, the king's forces subdued the Midlands, the West Country, Wales, and northern England. He organized his court at Oxford.

The Parliament had the edge over the Royalists since it was controlling London and therefore had the financial support for their army. Moreover, the navy assisted the Parliament, making it nearly impossible for the king to receive help from abroad. It also dominated the south-east and East Anglia.

Below are the most crucial events during the nine-year war between King Charles I and the Parliament:

The Siege of Portsmouth (September 7, 1642)

During the Civil War in 1642, Portsmouth's support was divided. The Mayor and most of the common folks aided the Parliament while the town's military governor, Colonel George Goring, supported the king and had command over the soldiers based in the town. The town itself was greatly fortified and equipped with 100 cannons and 1,400 barrels of gunpowder.

The Parliamentarian militia gathered at the north Portsea Island in order to prevent supplies getting into the town. There were many skirmishes between Goring's and the Parliament's forces. The last Royalist ship in Portsmouth harbor, the Henrietta Maria, was later captured by the group of Captain Browne Bushell.

Due to the pressure and lack of supplies, many of the Royalists surrendered. Sir William Waller's commissioners went to Portsmouth on August 28 for negotiation of peaceful surrender. However, Goring and his men refused the terms offered.

On September 2, the Parliamentarian forces at Gosport and Portsbridge bombarded the Royalist's hideout. The St. Thomas Church tower which served as a watchtower was heavily damaged. The next day, Colonel Richard Norton ambushed the strongpoint of Southsea Castle. Goring surrendered on September 7 and immediately left for the Netherlands.

Battle of Edgehill (October 23, 1642)

After King Charles fled from London, the country rapidly took sides—the conservative north aided the king while the south sympathized with the Parliament. The first battle of the Civil War had been a pitched battle. Had the royalists been more discipline, it could have also been the last.

The two opposing sides met at Edgehill in Warwickshire. The Parliamentarians were led by the Earl of Essex, Robert Devereux, while the Royalists were commanded by Prince Rupert, a veteran of the 30 Years War and the king's nephew.

Rupert initially turned the battle into their favor and made the Parliamentarian cavalry escape. However, instead of securing the victory, they chose to plunder the baggage train. In their absence, the opponent's remaining cavalry attacked their unit. The two sides were stalemates and gradually agreed to call it a draw. Charles retreated to Oxford, his winter base.

Roundaway Down 13th July 1643

Sir William Waller, a Parliamentary commander, managed to drive the Royalist army back to Devizes. Knowing that the Royalists were running off, with one company retreating into the direction of Salisbury, the commander let his troops relaxed before mounting a final attack on the Royalists. He failed to realize that the escaping troops turned north for reinforcements.

The Royalist reinforcements headed by Lord Henry Wilmot assisted the retreating forces. When Waller had seen that the Royalists were returning, he immediately assembled his army and assumed into battle position on Roundaway Down located at the north of Devizes. He positioned the cavalry at the sides and the infantry at the center.

The Royalists initiated the first attack which sent the Parliamentary cavalry fleeing. After that, Waller focused on Parliamentary infantry which firmly took their ground until another Royalist troop executed a sneak attack from behind. Caught sandwiched between two Royalist armies, many Parliamentarian soldiers escaped from the battlefield. The battle was won by the Royalist troops.

Battle of Newbury (September 20, 1643)

After the battle at Edgehill, the Royalists started to establish their control by seizing the majority of Yorkshire and winning battles in the West including the Adwalton Moor.

Robert Devereux, leading the only Parliamentarian army in the field, realized he was in trouble. He found that his supplies were dwindling, so he had to retreat back to London. However, the

Royalists blocked him at Newbury.

They engaged in a bitter battle on the first day. At midnight, when both sides decided to take a rest, both sides called their respective councils. The Parliamentarians were prepared to continue the battle despite their circumstances.

On the other hand, the Royalists decided to withdraw from the battle despite Prince Rupert's argument that they could win the battle. Unfortunately, he was outvoted. They missed their chance to annihilate the Parliamentarians and continued to suffer losses from then on.

The next morning, Robert felt relieved after discovering that the Royalists had left. The Parliamentarians returned to London where they were received with a hero's welcome.

Battle of Marston Moor (July 2, 1644)

The large-scale Civil War battle happened in Marston Moor and even marked a significant turning point. In 1944, the combined English Parliamentarian and Scottish forces sieged York. Charles immediately sent Prince Rupert's notorious cavalry to the rescue. Upon hearing that reinforcements were on the way, the Royalists abandoned the siege and gathered on Marston Moor.

However, the Parliamentarians brought in a new champion, an MP who had quickly risen through the ranks, Oliver Cromwell together with his Ironside cavalrymen. Cromwell built a reputation which rivaled Rupert's.

The numbers of men involved in Marston Moor were enough to call it the largest battle yet. It began at around seven o'clock p.m. and lasted for about two hours. In such a short period, approximately 4,000 Royalists were killed, and 1,500 were taken prisoners while the Parliamentarians and Scottish forces suffered 300 deaths.

The victory meant handing York and Northern England to the Parliamentarians. It also boosted the reputation of the Parliamentarians particularly the cavalry of Oliver Cromwell. It also shattered the myth of Rupert's invincibility and left the Royalist army in the north devastated.

Battle of Naseby (June 14, 1645)

Cromwell quickly established the New Model Army, a highly trained professional fighting force, after his victory in the Marston Moor. He, together with Thomas Fairfax, commanded this unit. This group practically won crucial battles specifically achieving a landmark battle at Naseby.

Prince Rupert's cavalry had achieved initial victory against the New Model Army but—again— lost when they had focused on looting the Parliamentarian baggage instead of securing their overall victory. This lack of discipline enabled the Parliamentarians to regroup and eventually defeat the Royalists. Upon Rupert's return, his cavalry already lost its will to fight. They lost the battle and with it, the war.

This loss marked the beginning of the end for King Charles himself. He lost his main army, and the Parliamentarians also apprehended correspondences showing that he was seeking Catholic help. Dressed as a servant, he fled from Oxford, on April 27, 1646, and surrendered to the Scottish forces at Newark.

The Fall of Charles I

The Royalists had a series of defeats from 1645 to 1646 through the alliance of both the Parliament and Scottish forces and the formation of Oliver Cromwell's New Model Army. Charles surrendered to the Scots who handed him over to the English Parliament. He got away and hid in the Isle of Wight in 1647. He tried to persuade dissatisfied Scots to invade.

The radical MPs including Cromwell were convinced that there would always be unrest as long as the king lived, so they put the king into a trial for high treason. King Charles was found guilty and was executed for treason on January 30, 1649, outside the Whitehall Banqueting House in London. His death concluded the English Civil War.

The Interregnum

Majority of the Parliament members wanted to convert the Church of England to Presbyterian. Moreover, they wanted that the attendance of church services should remain mandatory. However, the army disagreed because they wanted to have the freedom of worship.

In 1650, Charles II instigated another war having an arrangement with the Scots. Cromwell and his army headed to Scotland. At first, his campaign went rather badly as they were short of supplies and sickness spread in the ranks. In September 1650, he defeated the Scottish forces at Dunbar, killing 4,000 Scots and taking 10,000 prisoners before capturing the capital, Edinburgh. Cromwell then proceeded to the Firth of Forth, clearing the road to England along the way.

The Instrument of Government, a new constitution, was approved by the Council of Officers on December 15, 1653, and Oliver Cromwell was inaugurated as the Lord Protector the following day. At first, Cromwell ruled with a council, but in September 1654, he called for a new parliament. Unfortunately, the Protectorate Parliament rejected the Instrument of Government, so he dissolved it in January 1655.

In 1655, the country was divided into eleven districts wherein each was ruled by a Major-General. In 1656, another parliament assembly was called, but this time, some members were removed from the office. However, when the Parliament reconvened in January 1658, the excluded members in 1656 were reinstated. This time, the members criticized the new arrangements as they could not accept the newly nominated upper house. Their actions led Cromwell to dissolve the Parliament again in February 1658.

When Oliver Cromwell died on September 3, 1658, he was succeeded by his son, Richard, as Lord Protector. However, Richard had no power base from the Army and the Parliament. He resigned in May 1659.

The Long Parliament voted for its own dissolution in order to hold fresh elections for a new parliament which was later called the Convention Parliament. The new parliament then proclaimed that the government of England should be constituted by the King, Lords, and Commons.

The Parliament declared Charles II as the rightful English sovereign in 1660.

The Rule of Charles II: England in the Late 17th Century

During the reign of Charles II, the Parliament passed a series of four legal statutes (1661-1665) called the Clarendon Code. It aimed to re-establish the supremacy of the Anglican Church, persecuting the non-conformists or the Protestants who did not belong to the Church of England. The Corporation Act (1661) stated that all town officials should be a member of the Anglican Church.

In 1670, Charles created a secret treaty with King Louis XIV of France. It was known as the Treaty of Dover. By this, Louis promised to support Charles with money so he could no longer become dependent on the Parliament. In return, Charles had to join the French monarch in a war with Holland and that the English king had to announce that he was a Roman Catholic.

In 1672, Charles issued the Royal Declaration of Indulgence which suspends the law against the non-conformists. In 1673, the Parliament passed the Test Act which prohibited the Catholics as well as the non-conformists from holding a public office.

In 1679, the Parliament passed the Act of Habeas Corpus, making it illegal to imprison a person without a trial.

Charles had no legitimate children. When he died in 1685 at the age of 54, the throne was passed to his Catholic brother, James II.

The Glorious Revolution

In 1687, King James II presented a Declaration of Indulgence, preventing all laws against non-conformist Protestants and Catholics. The following year, he ordered the Church of England clergy to proclaim the declaration in the churches.

In June 1688, James had a son. The English could have been willing to tolerate James as long as he would not make his heir a Catholic. Despite this, he declared that his son would surely be brought up a Catholic. At his response, the Parliament declared the throne vacant.

Due to James religious tendencies and tyranny, he was removed from the throne through the Glorious Revolution in 1688. His daughter, Mary, and her husband, William of Orange, were then declared as the new monarchs.

Mary and William were "invited" by the Protestant aristocracy to lead an invasion from the Netherlands. They soon overcame James' troops at the Battle of the Boyne. They let the king flee away to France where he lived for the rest of his life under the shelter of King Louis XIV.

The new English monarchs were later called the "Grand Alliance." The Parliament then officially approved that all the future kings and queens of the country would have to be Protestant. Upon the death of

William in 1702 (Mary died earlier in 1694), James II's second daughter, Anne, was crowned queen.

In 1707, the Act of Union joined the English and Scottish Parliaments in order to create a unified Kingdom of Great Britain. It also declared London as the center of political power.

Queen Anne died in 1714, leaving no heir. Her distant German cousin, George of Hanover, was then summoned to rule the kingdom.

Chapter 7: Georgian Era (1660-1830)

The Georgian era spans from 1714 to 1830, being named after the four Georges of the Hanoverian house and is often extended to include William IV's reign which ended upon his death in 1837. The term "Georgian" is often used as reference to the architecture, social, and political history of that particular period.

The Georgian era witnessed the rise of Britain as a global power, establishing itself as the center of the growing empire. The change occurred in the 1770s under the rule of George III as the world's first industrialized country. The period was defined by its extreme luxury and poverty.

The inauguration of the Kingdom of Great Britain in 1707 signaled the new British identity celebrated by the Rule Britannia anthem (1740), the British Museum foundation (1753), and the Encyclopedia Britannica publication (1768). However, England was still able to keep its own unique character during the early Georgian era. Its refined style, etiquette, arts, architecture, and literature strongly contrasted with the uncouth Georgian mode like casual violence, extreme sports, poverty, and epidemic addition in gin. Handel's oratorios prospered at the same time as the infamous debauchery practices as told by his friend, William Hogarth.

George I

When Queen Anne died in 1714, she was succeeded by her German and Protestant relative, George I of Hanover. Since he couldn't even speak English, the new British monarch soon faced opposition from the Jacobites who supported the restoration of the Catholic Stuarts into the throne. However, the rebellions were mainly concentrated in Scotland and were suppressed by the end of the year.

The monarch turned to the help of the Whigs since the Tories were rather sympathetic to the Jacobites. The contention eventually involved his only son, the Prince of Wales, and worsened their already sour relationship.

George I actively campaigned in British foreign policies. His sharp diplomatic judgment helped him establish an anti-Spanish alliance with France in 1717-1718.

When the South Sea Company collapsed in 1720, despite the heavy royal, aristocratic, and government investments, the kingdom faced dire economic crisis. This event resulted in the installment of Robert Walpole as the first Lord of the Treasury in April 1721. His position can also be identified as the Prime Minister. Together with his ascension comes the decline of the popularity of the monarchy. With this, George became detached from his involvement in the government.

George I continued to be unfavorable in the eyes of his subjects for the remainder of his life partly because of his inability to speak in English and mainly because of ugly rumors concerning his treatment of his wife and the notoriety of his German mistresses.

When George died in Hanover on June 11, 1727, he was succeeded by his son.

George II

George II was also German-born just like the previous monarch. He held the titles Archtreasurer and Prince Elector of the Holy Roman Empire along with his title as the Sovereign of Great Britain and England. He was considered as a powerful ruler and practically the last British ruler to personally lead his troops in the battle at Dettingen in 1743. George Frideric Hander, a celebrated Baroque composer, was commissioned to create his coronation anthem, "Zadok the Priest," which has since been played in every British coronation.

George II considerably expanded the British Empire during his rule.

His achievements included the development of the Gregorian calendar and replacing the Julian calendar by 1752. Since then, the New Year was officially moved from March 25 to January 1.

King George's War (1740- 1748)

In 1740, the deaths of two European sovereigns embarked the continent into war. King Frederick William I was succeeded by his son when he died on May 31, 1740. Frederick, known as ruthlessly ambitious, also inherited the most progressive army in the whole of Europe and the most efficient bureaucratic government institutions his father developed. These elements helped Frederick (historically known as "Frederick the Great").

On October 19, 1740, Emperor Charles VI of Austria died leaving the throne to his daughter, Maria Theresa. Since Charles thought that his daughter would find a hard time defending the throne, he spent the last years of his life designing the *Pragmatic Sanction of Prague*, a convention that assured Maria Theresa's imperial dominions, coercing other European monarchs to sign it. Unfortunately, Frederick's miscalculation.

The Prussian heir broke its commitment and immediately seized Silesia, appropriating the rich Austrian province as part of his kingdom. He completely underestimated the Austrian monarch who instantly declared war on Prussia, invaded Silesia and turned the whole Continent against him. The war was only concluded in the 1764 Treaty of Paris, confirming Prussia's ownership of Silesia.

In the early phase of the war (1740-1748), Prussia and Austria fought in Silesia and Bohemia while the French invaded Bavaria. The French proceeded to threaten the Netherlands, prompting the Pragmatic Army (from the Pragmatic Sanction) to assemble in order to counter the French forces. The army consisted of the Austrian and German militia—including the Hanover, the jurisdiction of George II.

King George sent his English troops to join the Pragmatic Allies, ready to fight not just for the Austrian monarch but to defend his beloved Hanover. The English troops were dispatched to Flanders in mid-1742 and stationed there until 1748. They fought four battles: Dettingen (1743), Fontenoy (1745), Rocoux (1746), and Lauffeldt (1747).

On June 16, 1743, the Pragmatic Army headed south to Frankfurt, Germany. There, George II joined them and fought the Battle of Dettingen against the French forces of the Duc de Noailles.

In early 1745, the Duke of Cumberland, King George's favorite son, became the Pragmatic Army's commander-in-chief. He led the army to the City of Tournai which was then sieged by Marshal Saxe. This went down in history as the Battle of Fontenoy.

After a brief interlude in 1746, the British resumed their help in the battles of Roucoux and Lauffeldt, and the war ceased in 1746 although it was considered as the calm before the storm, the Seven Years' War in 1755.

The Jacobite Rising (1745)

The last Jacobite rebellion, also known as the *Forty-five Rebellion*, was the most formidable among the Jacobite dispute for the throne. The prospect in 1745 looked hopeless even if the rising this time comprised of fewer Scottish Highlanders compared to the 1715 revolution. However, the daring young prince, Charles Edward (historically known as the Young Pretender and Bonnie Prince Charlie) who motivated the rebels to get as far as Derby and the absence of the government militia led to a serious insurgency.

In a matter of a few weeks, Charles earned the sympathies of Scotland and even became the victor of Prestonpans (September 21). He won the Battle of Falkirk Muir on January 17, 1746, and retreated to the Highlands. However, the Duke of Cumberland, William

77

August, was able to suppress their forces on April 16 at the Battle of Culloden located near Inverness. At least 80 rebels were executed while the escapees were hunted down and arbitrarily killed or driven into exile. The government tried to track Charles down, but he was able to escape to the Continent on September 20, 1746.

The Seven Years' War (1753-1763)

Britain played a major role in the Seven Years' War and emerged as the top colonial power, having gained new territories through the Treaty of Paris (1763) and established itself as the world's leading naval power.

At first, the odds were against Great Britain which suffered many deaths due to the plague, scurvy and the French forces in North America (1754-1755). They even lost Menorca in 1756. Their major ally, Austria, switched sides with France, so they have to immediately establish ties with their former opponent, Prussia. However, things changed in 1759 which signaled the beginning of what the British call *Annus Mirabilis* (or the "Year of Miracles"). They won numerous battles beginning with their success over the French in Germany, North America (New France), and in India. In 1761, they had a conflict with Spain. The following year, the British forces were able to capture the western and eastern capitals of the Spanish Empire, Havana (Cuba) and Manila (Philippines). They were also able to stave off the Spanish forces from Portugal.

George III

George III, the first Hanoverian King to speak English as his first language, succeeded the British throne in 1760 at the age of 22. In addition to the crown, he also inherited the ongoing world war (Seven Years' War), changing social issues, and religious discord. Despite all of these, he defeated France during the Seven Years' War, Great Britain rose up as a dominant European power in India and

North America and led a successful resistance against the Napoleonic forces in 1815. He was also the longest living British monarch before Queen Victoria and Queen Elizabeth II.

Early Reign

In 1761, King George was married to the daughter of a German duke, Charlotte of Mecklenburg-Strelitz. Although it was a political union, George remained faithful to his wife and sired 15 children with her.

George III worked hard to accelerate the end of the Seven Years' War, forcing William Pitt the Elder, the British war minister who wanted to extend the conflict, to resign. The following year, the king appointed his former tutor, John Stuart, Earl of Bute, as his Prime Minister. The earl became the main influence in the early stages of the king's reign. However, he was forced to resign due to the alleged sex scandal with the Dowager Princess of Wales, the mother of George III.

In 1764, the new minister George Grenville initiated the Stamp Act, a means of raising revenue in British America. The decree was vehemently opposed in America, particularly by the pamphleteers whose paper was also included in the taxation. The Parliament repealed the act two years later, but the mistrust generated still persisted in the colonies.

The American Revolution

In 1770, Frederick North (popularly known as "Lord North") became the Prime minister. The event also marked the beginning of a twelve-year period of parliamentary stability. Three years after his inauguration, he introduced an act taxing tea in the British colonies. The Americans responded with a strong complaint of taxation without representation and soon organized what was famously known as the Boston Tea Party. However, the Prime Minister held on to his decision since he had the king's support.

On April 19, 1775, the American Revolution started with the Battles of Lexington and Concord. The following year, the Declaration of Independence depicted the British king as a tyrant who foolishly misused his rights to govern the colonies. Little did they know that the Parliament—and not the crow—was the actual decision-making body for colonial policies even though George had direct and indirect influence over them.

In 1781, Britain was defeated at Yorktown. The king drafted an abdication speech but decided to go with the Parliament's idea of peace negotiations. The Treaty of Paris in 1783 recognized the United States and relinquished Florida to Spain.

Later Rule and Mental Illness

In 1778, George experienced violent bouts of insanity which required him to be restrained with a straitjacket. He underwent various treatments for months. Because of this, Great Britain experienced a temporary political crisis. Fortunately, he recovered a year later and reigned for another 12 years. His popularity even rose after this ordeal, and he became a symbol of stability amidst the period of France's revolutionary chaos.

In 1804, the British monarch suffered insanity for the second time although he recuperated immediately. However, he succumbed to his fatal illness in 1810 so his son, George IV had to become the prince regent. George IV displayed characteristics of a promising monarch as he defeated Napoleon in the Battle of Waterloo in 1815.

George III died mad, blind, and deaf on January 29, 1820. The cause of his death was unknown although it might have been caused by porphyria or arsenic poisoning according to the 2005 analysis of hair samples.

George IV

George IV was the eldest son of George III and Charlotte Sophia of Mecklenburg-Strelitz. He became the sovereign de facto during his father's illness before he was finally crowned as the king of Great Britain and Ireland on January 29, 1820, at the age of 58.

George IV described himself as someone "rather too fond of women and wine." His lifestyle and friendship with Charles James fox together with other hedonistic politicians made his father regard him with contempt. In 1784, he met the only woman he ever loved, Maria Fitzherbert. They were secretly married on the 15th of December, 1785 but the contract was later declared invalid since the members of the royal family under 25 were prohibited to marry without the king's consent.

In order to persuade the Parliament to pay his debts, George IV was forced to commit into a loveless marriage on April 8, 1795, with Caroline, the daughter of the Duke of Brunswick. However, the couple immediately separated only a few weeks after their only child, Princess Charlotte, was born. Caroline returned from Italy in 1820, just a few months after George ascended to the throne in order to claim her rights as the queen consort. However, a bill from the House of the Lords deprived her of those rights on the grounds of adultery. Caroline died the following year due to cancer although some rumors say that she had been poisoned.

In 1810, when his father, George III, yielded to his sanity, George IV rose as the regent under the Regency Act. When the statute expired, he decided to continue employing his father's ministers instead of appointing new ministers from among his old Whig friends. This was considered as a great decision as it benefited the whole of Europe because the 2nd Earl Grey and other top Whigs had prepared to abandon their war with France and let Napoleon take over the continent. In 1815, the British defeated Napoleon and his forces.

George IV's character was partly enhanced by his linguistic prowess and other intellectual abilities particularly his shrewd judgment in arts. During his lifetime, he served as the benefactor of John Nash, the architect who developed the Regent Street and Regent's Park in London; and sponsored Sir Jeffry Wyatville's rehabilitation of the Windsor Castle. His most popular achievement was the Royal Pavilion at Brighton with its Chinese and Mughal Indian ornamentation designed by John Nash.

William IV

Known as *Silly Billy* and the *Sailor King*, William IV was king of Great Britain and Ireland from 1830. William was born at Buckingham Palace, London on August 21, 1765, as the third son of George III and Queen Charlotte. He joined the Royal Navy at a young age of 13. He enjoyed his voyages, performing his services in America and the West Indies. He became an admiral in 1811.

When the only daughter of King George IV had died in 1818, the king's brothers hastily married in order to produce heirs. That same year, William married Princess Adelaide of Saxe-Meiningen. With the death of his brother in 1830, William ascended the throne.

Initially, the newly crowned king was very popular. His humility to take a simple coronation heavily contrasted the extravagance during the reign of his elder brother. However, William's reign was dominated by the Reform crisis. It started soon after the Duke of Wellington's Tory government, which William backed up, was defeated during the general election in 1830.

Lord Grey who led the Whigs rose up into power and immediately worked on the electoral reform against powerful opposition in Peers and Commons. In the 1831 general election, many in the Commons had given their support to the Whigs while the Peers continued to reject the Reform Bill. In the winter of 1831 to 1832, Great Britain faced a political crisis, and there were riots in some parts of the country.

Eventually, the king conceded to create enough new Whig peers to get the bill through the House of Lords who finally passed it. The 1832 Reform Act repealed some of the worst oppressions of the electoral system and even incorporated the authorization to the middle classes.

When King William IV died on June 20, 1837, he had no surviving children so his niece, Victoria succeeded him. His death also marked the end of the Gregorian era.

Chapter 8: The British Empire and Victorian Era (1837-1901)

At 18, Victoria, niece of William IV, inherited the throne and crowned queen when his uncle died of liver disease in 1837.

Originally, Victoria should have succeeded the throne of the kingdom of Hanover, but because of the Salic Law which excludes females from succeeding Hanover's throne, she was disqualified as heiress to the kingdom.

Victoria as Queen

Queen Victoria (1819-1901), while still living, was the first English monarch to have the period of her reign named in her honor.

Owing to the facts that she never thought of being queen, unmarried and inexperienced of politics, she relied on Lord Melbourne (1779-1847), her prime minister as to whom the city of Australia was named after.

She eventually married her first cousin, Prince Albert of Saxe-Coburg- Goth (1819-1861). Both of them were King Leopold I of Saxe-Coburg-Gotha's (King of Belgium) niece and nephew.

Victorian Era

From medical, technological and scientific knowledge, advancement to location change and population growth, fast developmental progress and changes were prime characteristics of the Victorian Age. It was also an age that started in confidence and optimism that led to economic expansion and prosperity that transformed and deeply affected the country's disposition. Over time, it gave way to uncertainty and doubt to Britain's world standing.

As of today, the 19th century is associated with religious observation, family ethics, institutional faith, and Protestant work ethics.

In 1851, Prince Albert organized the first world fair or known as The Great Exhibition. The proceeds were used for building the South Kensington Museum in London. Later, its name was changed into the Victoria and Albert Museum.

Britain asserted its influence and domination almost everywhere around the world that resulted in numerous wars such as:

- Boer Wars with the Dutch-speaking settlers of South Africa (1880-1981 and 1899-1902)
- Opium Wars with Qing China (1839-1942 and 1856-1960)

Also, the United Kingdom was alongside the Ottoman Empire versus Russia in 1854 and was brought to the Crimean War (1854-1856). One of the most prominent figures of that war was Florence Nightingale (1820-1910) who pioneered modern nursing and fought for women's condition to improve.

At the age of 42, Prince Albert died an untimely death in 1861 that devastated Queen Victoria. The latter retired in a semi-permanent mourning state. But nevertheless, she was involved in a romantic relationship with John Brown (1826-1883), her Scottish servant. In fact, there were even rumors of a secret marriage happening between the two which became the object of the film: Mrs. Brown.

The latter years of the Victorian reign remained under the control of two prime ministers, namely:

Benjamin Disraeli (1808-1881) who was the Queen's favorite. In 1876, he crowned Queen Victoria as Empress of India. In return, he was made Earl of Beaconsfield.

William Ewart Gladstone (1809-1898) was the rival of Disraeli. He was liberal and often in dissonance with the Queen and Disraeli.

Between 1868-1894, he enjoyed the strong support of his party that enabled him to stay in power for 14 years. He advocated both universal education and universal suffrage for men. He also legalized trade unions.

Large and patriarchal, the majority of the 19th-century families encouraged respectability, social differences, hard work, and religious conformity. Even though this kind of lifestyle was often contested by its contemporaries, still, it was well- grounded and effective. Educational and employment opportunities for women that were usually portrayed as whores or Madonnas increased, and they were also given roles aside from their common roles in the family.

Because Victorians value politics much, they believed in exporting their evolved representative government throughout the British Empire as to which they also believed it to be perfect. This era birthed and spread political movements such as liberalism, organized feminism and socialism.

Geographical explorations by the opening up of Asia to the west and Africa gave excitement to British Victorians, but due to the continuous defiance of Ireland and the humiliation from failures of the Boer War, they were distracted. But still, British Supremacy remained unchallenged at sea throughout the century.

Work and play expanded dramatically at the peak of the Victorian Era. Travel and leisure opportunities for all were stimulated by the national railway network. Race meetings, football matches and visits to seaside resorts were enjoyed by the urban society. Literacy increased, popular journalism was embraced, and novel ascended and became the most powerful and popular icon. Significant changes in medicine, accompanied by specialization and developments in surgery, and hospital infrastructures were made possible due to scientific thought progress in the 19th century. Medical breakthroughs in anesthetics were distinguished and publicized by the Queen herself after she took chloroform for the birthing of her son in 1853; and in antiseptics as introduced by Joseph Lister (1827-1912).

The growth of hospitals, construction of asylums, and specialized workhouses for the most vulnerable members of the society was eagerly accepted by the public, and their faith to the said institutions was evident.

The longest and most glorious reign that any British monarch ever had was ascribed to Queen Victoria. She reigned 64 years, and she ruled 40% of the world and was a queen to a quarter of the world's entire population.

Chapter 9: The Word Wars and Aftermath (18th-20th Century)

World War I (1914-1918)

The First World War or World War I is a series of battles between the Allies (which consists of France, Belgium, Russia, Serbia, and Great Britain) and Central Powers (Germany and Austria-Hungary). In commoner's viewpoint, most think that there is no need for Britain to go to war. However, English historians, as well as other experts, simply didn't agree with that.

The main reason why Britain had to go to war is the fact that it had a 'Gentleman's Agreement' of some sort with France and Belgium, which is a neutral country during that time. For the Germans, the best and fastest route to Paris is none other than Belgium itself, bringing that country up as a strategic target for an invasion. They also have their eyes in Iran, which supplies the oil for the British Navy. And to make matters worse for Britain, the Ottoman Turks also joined the Central Powers during that time, forcing the British to make plans in defending the Suez Canal, which lead to the Persian Oil fields as well as India.

Having considerably lower numbers in soldiers compared to their allies during that time, the British shipped native Indian forces from their subcontinent as Chinese volunteers in order to provide sufficient men for the Western European troops. Later on, troops from New Zealand, Australia, and Egypt also joined the war, supporting Britain's war efforts.

Trench Warfare

One of the most notable events during the First World War is none other than trench warfare. Due to the fact that the Central Powers use the breech-loading rifle as well as the fast and deadly machine gun, fighting them, head-on is just a stupid move. Because of this, the Allied soldiers decided to dig trenches in order to protect themselves from the incoming gunfire. These trenches became more important after the invention of accurate field guns, hence making trench-digging a very important skill in the military even nowadays.

For the first three months, the Germans marched so fast that it became almost impossible for soldiers in Paris to finish digging up defensive trenches. What made them survive the ordeal, however, is the fact that there was still no motorized transportation such as jeepneys and motorcycles during that time, delaying the German's transport of ammunition as well as provisions for the entire war. And since the battle theatre is in the French capital, the soldiers used their trains when transporting their cargo as well as reinforcements, making it possible for them to drive the Germans away.

Pushed back towards their own border, the Germans also made use of trenches as defensive measures and improved it according to their own taste and style. This led to more intense trench warfare, increasing the number of casualties on both sides. Because of this, the British also made adjustments by conscripting coal miners in the second half of the war, whose aims is to dig right under Germans' defensive lines and blowing enemy soldiers away along with their trenches.

World War I Aftermath

The outcome of the First World War dramatically changed the face of entire Europe. Aside from the suffering economy as well as deaths on both sides, the losers literally lost everything, which was seen in the collapse of both the Austro-Hungarian and Turkish Ottoman Empire, which reigned for more than four centuries. Because of this, new countries were founded and rose in the Middle East, namely Iraq, Saudi Arabia, Jordan, Syria, and Israel. The Germans, on the other hand, also lost most of their territory, even forcing themselves to give most of East Prussia to Poland. France also forced them to pay for all the damages they caused.

Russia didn't survive the war, either. Despite it being a part of the Allied Forces, the country not only lost a significant number of men; it also lost most of its treasury, eventually making it hard to sustain its citizens. Because of this, many peasants and their families in St. Petersburg starved to death, forcing the citizens, bourgeoisie and the middle class to assassinate the Tsar and found the Union of Soviet Socialist Republics under the communist Vladimir Lenin.

World War II

Being forced to pay for the damages they caused during the First World War, the German economy suffered much, making them start another one, which was later known as the Second World War or World War II.

Known to be a strong country, Britain not only defended their homeland as well as their territories from the Germans. This time, the Germans under the dictatorship of Adolf Hitler also had two other troublesome allies in the form of Italy and Japan, forming the so-called Rome-Berlin-Tokyo Axis. The British, on the other hand, had its whole empire, Russia, China, and the USA as members of the Allies.

On the 3rd day of September 1939, the British along with France declared war against Hitler and Nazi Germany under Anglo-Polish Military Alliance because of their Blitzkrieg invasion of Poland and having annexed Czechoslovakia (Ceylon) Austria and Rhineland.

Setting his eyes from the Atlantic to Moscow, Adolf Hitler wants to conquer all of Europe. At the same time, the Japanese under Emperor Hirohito also wanted to gain control of Asia under the so-called 'Greater East Asia Co-Prosperity Sphere.' The British also have to secure their hold in Asia since the Japanese have their eyes on Burma and Malaysia, which happened to supply Britain with rubber as well as oil.

By September 9, the British landed in France, providing military support. What they don't know, however, is that the Germans had an agreement with the Russians to attack Poland simultaneously. Because of this, Poland has fallen in a span of one month.

According to historians, Hitler did not really intend to attack Britain at first, due to the fact that he simply respected the country and the reigning Queen of England was known to have German origins. What changed his mind, however, is that he simply cannot trust Winston Churchill, who recently became prime minister. In addition to that, he was afraid that Britain and the USA would possibly join forces and attack him in the process. This is the reason why the Germans started attacking London mostly via air raids on July 3, 1940, which lasted for three months. But despite all of these, the British successfully resisted the invasion, forcing Hitler and Nazi Germany to give up his plan on October 12, 1940.

World War II Aftermath

Because of the war, almost all of Europe except Ireland was in ruins, particularly Britain having exchanged blows with the Germans for five long years. Under the so-called Marshall Plan, the Americans acted as the bank, financing the countries that needed money the most for their reconstruction and re-stabilization of their economy. Despite their evil deeds, the Germans became the primary beneficiaries for this due to the fact that the country's economic collapse was the reason behind the Second World War.

Chapter 10: Modern England in the 21st Century

Geography

As a country that is now a part of the United Kingdom of Great Britain, England shared land borders with Scotland to the north-northwest and Wales to the west. Lying on the west of England is the Irish Sea and the Celtic Sea to the southwest. Separated from Continental Europe by the English Channel to the south and the North Sea to the east, England covers about five-eighths of the whole island of Great Britain sitting in the North Atlantic and includes more than a hundred of smaller islands.

The country's terrain mostly consisted of low hills and plains especially on its southern and central parts while there is mountainous terrain in the North such as the Lake District and Pennines and in the West, the Shropshire Hills and Dartmoor.

London is considered the capital of England with the largest metropolitan area in both the United Kingdom and the European Union.

The Kingdom of England including Wales ceased being a separate and distinct sovereign state on the 1st of May 1707 when the Acts of Union implemented the Treaty of the Union creating a political union with the Kingdom of Scotland - the United Kingdom of Great Britain and Ireland. In 1922, the Irish Free State formally withdraw from the United Kingdom which led to it being renamed the United Kingdom of Great Britain and Northern Ireland.

The Transition

In the early 21st century, England continuously progressed from an industrial society where most people were employed in the manufacturing and mining industries to work in service industries. By 2011, about 80 percent of the labor force work service-related jobs.

At the beginning of the century, unemployment was relatively low at 5.5%, but it sharply increased since the recession in 2008 until it reached 8% in 2011. It only decreased again at 4.3% in 2017 after the Great Recession.

England's population grew mainly because of immigration. In 2001, the population reached 52 million, by 2013 it increased to 63.7 million, and in 2018, it grew to approximately 66 million.

Meanwhile, the internet greatly influenced the lives of more than half of the households in England by 2006. In 2018, about 90 percent of the households had access to the internet. This revolution is expected to lead to another kind of movement. Emails and social networking have played a key role in communication and people's lifestyle. Business transactions like banking and shopping can be done online. Even gaming and entertainment can be done via the internet.

The English Economy

At present, the English economy strongly relies on services with the main industries include education, music, travel, fashion, food, and luxury cars. Here is the list of the top money-makers in each industry field:

- Education: Oxford University and Cambridge University (plus hundreds of English language schools)
- Music: EMI Records Ltd., HMV, Virgin Records, Warner Music

- Travel: Virgin Atlantic, British Airways, Costsaver, Trafalgar
- Clothes and Fashion: Burberry, Vivienne Westwood, Dunhill, Paul Smith, Hackett, New & Lingwood
- Food: Cadbury-Schweppes, Unilever, KitKat
- Luxury Cars: Aston Martin, Rolls Royce, Bentley, MG, McLaren, Lotus, Jaguar, Bentley
- Brexit: Leaving the European Union

In mid-2016, the British people voted to leave the European Union (EU) by a 52% to 48% margin. This led to huge consequences concerning Britain, the whole of Europe, and the global economy.

In 1973, Britain joined the European Economic Community and the EU in the 1990s. However, Britain never completely acknowledged the legitimacy of the union's control over the British institutions just like the other members did. For instance, Britain refused to adopt the common currency or join the Schengen Area which removes internal border controls.

Since the start of the Great Recession in 2008, Britain's background skepticism greatly intensified due to the poor performance of European economies. The continent took the recession hard and even had a hard time recovering.

Two of the leading common arguments in favor of Brexit concentrated on the EU's inconvenient economic regulations and the liberal rules for internal migration. Even advocates like Boris Johnson, the mayor of London during that time, criticized the continuously growing power of the unelected EU bureaucrats in Brussels. He pointed out that the increasing "works" of the EU negatively affect the nation's decision-making. He was talking about rules like prohibiting the recycling of a teabag, that children below eight years old shouldn't be allowed to blow balloons or there should be a limit on the power of vacuum cleaners. Such regulations were deemed importunate and extremely undemocratic.

Constitutional Framework

England itself does not have its own formal government and constitution for it operates on a nationwide British basis. We may give credit to the English for the evolution of Parliament which has been related to the Anglo-Saxon practice of regular gatherings in its medieval form. The English are likewise credited for the success of the Revolution of 1688 which affirmed the freedom of speech, parliamentary control of the army and taxation, the rule of law, and religious toleration. Unlike Wales, Scotland, and Northern Ireland which all have their own assembly of parliament, the regional government never exists in England.

Local Government

England has a distinct form of local government which has evolved through the centuries, Historic counties or shires that were developed during the Anglo-Saxon still continue as geographic, administrative, and local units. It was in 1888 that the Local Government Act regulated the administrative functions of these counties and redrawn some of the boundaries to create new administrative counties including the country of London which is formed from parts of the historic counties of Kent, Surrey, and Middlesex.

Culture

England's contribution to the world and the United Kingdom of Great Britain is countless and numerous with its culture too vast for anything. Historically, England is a country of homogenous origin and developed coherent traditions, but as the British Empire expanded and expanded people from all over the globe, the English culture has been blended with diverse contributions from Asians, Afro-Caribbean, Muslims, and other immigrant groups. Other areas of the United Kingdom had likewise experienced the same cultural and social diversification. With these similarities, England is not always distinguishable from Scotland, Wales, and Northern Ireland.

The former insularity of English life was replaced by a cosmopolitan familiarity with exotic things. Italian, Chinese, and Indian cuisines became a natural part of some meals being offered in restaurants just as guitar-based rocks naturally blends with Afro-Caribbean salsa and South Asian rap.

Although England has become ever more diverse culturally, it continues to exert a strong cultural influence on the rest of the world. English films, music, and literature garnered wide audiences all over the world as the English language has become a preferred international medium of cultural and economic change.

Social Customs and Daily Life

English daily life and customs in rural and urban areas show a significant difference. Much of the English literature explores the difference between life in a town and country as well as the comparison of being on a farm or factory.

Today, even though the English had traveled much to other parts of the world, yet their ties to the rural past remains strong and evident. Those who have been used to living in urban areas usually retire to villages and country cottages. Even in the smallest home in an urban, one is most likely to find a garden.

There are many holidays in England that is likewise celebrated throughout the world like Christmas. Christmas for the English is less a commercial event than an opportunity for festive gathering and singing.

Remembrance Day has held every November 11 in honor of British soldiers who died in World War I. There are also remembrances that are distinct to the English and inexplicable to outsiders including:

- St. George's Day (April 23) - honors England patron saint
- Guy Fawkes Night (November 5) –is held in commemoration of a Roman Catholic conspiracy to blow up the Houses of Parliament in 1605.

St. George's Day is hardly celebrated in England contrary to patron saint's celebrations in Ireland, Wales, and Scotland. This lack of official celebration for St. George's Day contributes to the ambiguity of being English as distinguished from being British.

A military parade called "Trooping the Colour" commemorates in the summer to celebrate the monarch's birthday. This has been a practice since the 18th century.

Food and Cuisine

English cuisines are mostly based on pork, chicken, fish, beef, and lamb traditionally served with potatoes and another vegetable with minimal embellishments. For fish-based cuisine which usually used cod or haddock, these are deep fried in batter and served with deep-fried potato chips.

When English is traveling home, the most popular carryout dishes are fish and chips usually wrapped in old newspapers to keep them warm.

It is also normal especially for middle-income families to have the Sunday joint as the main meal of the week. The Sunday joint is a substantial piece of pork, beef or lamb roasted in the oven in the morning and served at midday. However, this tradition changed around the 1950s and 1960s when immigrants from China and India arrived bringing with them their own distinctive cuisines. Chinese and Indian restaurants then became a familiar sight in almost all parts of England.

The American fast-food chains started dotting the landscape, and the rapid post-World War II growth of holiday travel to Europe particularly to Spain, Greece, France, and Italy helped exposed the English to new foods, variations, flavors, and ingredients. Many of these had found their way into a new generation of cookbooks filling up the typical English kitchen.

Literature

England has attained the most influential cultural expression in its literature. Each stage in the development of the English language has produced its masterworks for more than a millennium.

Before the arrival of the Anglo-Saxons, little is known of the English literature though echoes of the Celtic pasts are echoed in Arthurian legend. The Anglo-Saxon literature presented in the Old English language is a remarkable diverse work of art. Surviving pieces include corpus hymns, lyric poems, songs, riddles and spells dating back from the 9th to the 10th century.

Following the Norman conquest of 1066, the French help shaped the vocabulary and the literary preoccupations of Middle English. Geoffrey Chaucer displayed both the earth vernacular and the philosophical concerns of this period in Canterbury Tales and Troilus and Criseyde. On the other hand, Piers Plowman of William Langland was an early expression of political and religious dissent that later characterized English literature.

The Elizabethan era in the late 16th century fostered the flourishing Renaissance and the golden age of the English literature. William Shakespeare's popular plays apparently represent the culmination of the Elizabethan English but somehow were able to achieve a depth of characterization and richness of invention that had fixed them in the dramatic repertoire of almost every language.

The 1611 publication of the King James Version of the Bible has blended the literature of the period with a remarkably vigorous language and religious imagery while serving as an important tool in spreading literacy throughout England.

The 17th century long lists of conflicts in both religious and political aspects provided a backdrop for a treasure of poetry.

Music

Musical arts in England can be traced back to plainsong and were later blended with the help of monks and troubadours who were traveling throughout Europe which freely intermingled and spread out quickly in many regions.

England was able to produce notable producers including:

- John Dowland
- Thomas Tallis
- Thomas Morley
- William Byrd

Baroque composers George Frideric Handel and Henry Purcell established musical stature remain unquestioned.

Sports and Recreation

While England has a vigorous and lively cultural life, its commerce is increasingly concentrating on the exploitation of leisure from gambling, tourists holiday package tours, and transformation of the traditional English pub through trendy interior decorations.

Weekends are usually spent on countryside trips and for outdoor activities from hiking, fishing, and mountaineering. England manages to share to the world some sports including cricket, rugby, soccer, and football but now failed to outshine other nations in international competitions. Although England participates in sports like basketball, angling, snooker, and swimming, yet most preferred leisure activities are connected with home activities.

Elizabeth II: The Longest Reigning Monarch

On September 9, 2015, at exactly 5:30 p.m. (BST), Queen Elizabeth II became the longest-serving British monarch, surpassing her ancestor, Queen Victoria. According to BBC, the queen had served the country for 23,226 days and about 16.5 hours. Yet that day, the 89-year-old queen chose to simply enjoy the day doing her queenly duty by inaugurating the Scottish Borders Railway in Scotland.

The following year, on October 13, Elizabeth II became the world's longest reigning sovereign after the death of King Bhumibol Adulyadej of Thailand.

Conclusion

Referring to the history of England, it is difficult to separate it from the history of Britain. Since the arrival of the Anglo-Saxons into the Roman's Britannia in the early part of the 5th century A.D. up to the time of the Unions that bound England, Wales, Scotland, Ireland, and the Northern Ireland, the history of England is complicated and intricately interwoven with that of the British Isles.

The name of the country and the word "English" is 'taken from the Old English word for "Angles" while "British" and "Britain" are derived from a Roman term for the inhabitants' language of the British Isles called "Brythonic" or "p-Celtic."

For non-English, it would be very difficult to distinguish which are British and which is English. With the union of countries unified under the United Kingdom of Great Britain and Northern Ireland, these countries had lost their own national identities although the English language was more identified with the English than the British – although they are one.

Religion played a significant role in the formation of the history of England with Catholicism and Protestantism serving as major tools in the powerplay of significant figures. The long lists of successions side by side with unending struggles, violence, and life's dramas added to the configuration of political and religious settings.

Today, these two dominant factions managed to work separately ignoring what had happened in the past although we can't deny that each one still bears each own organizational power and influence.

Regardless of the past and internal struggles, England remained and will always be a strong and formidable force to reckon with. Its long lists of influences, powers, challenges, turmoil, and struggles embedded in its historical saga are not something that can easily be forgotten. No one can deny the fact that England was one of the world's formidable forces the world ever had.

Made in the USA
San Bernardino, CA
10 June 2019